BOB LECHTRECK

'M OK, YOU'RE A PAIN IN THE NECK

*Other books by Albert Vorspan*

MY RABBI DOESN'T MAKE HOUSE CALLS

SO THE KIDS ARE REVOLTING . . . ?

MAZEL TOV! YOU'RE MIDDLE-AGED

*Albert Vorspan*

# I'm OK, You're a
# Pain in the Neck

*1976*

*Doubleday & Company, Inc., Garden City, New York*

Library of Congress Cataloging in Publication Data

Vorspan, Albert.
  I'm OK, you're a pain in the neck.

    1. Self-actualization (Psychology)—Anecdotes, facetiae, satire, etc. I.
Title.
PN6231.P785V6      818'.5'407
ISBN 0-385-04011-3
Library of Congress Catalog Card Number 75-21248

This book is dedicated to Alex Liepa, my editor.

We get along famously because we have virtually nothing in common. He is a Lutheran, originally from Latvia, politically conservative; I am a Litvak, Reform Jew, originally from Minnesota and a flaming liberal. He lives on the North Shore of Long Island; I on the South. He thinks I am funny when I am serious, and he thinks I am serious when I am funny.

But he is a skilled editor who knows a great manuscript when he sees one. Nevertheless, he keeps publishing me and, with patience and perseverance, he has teased more books out of me than I knew I had in me.

Alex is OK, even though he is a pain in the neck.

# PROLOGUE

That feisty philosopher, Epictetus, pointed out, thousands of years ago, that we have practically no control over the activities of other people, so why don't we cool it and concentrate on getting our own heads on straight? We have nowhere to go but up.

Shakespeare, in similar vein, laid it on us in iambic pentameter yet, thusly: "To thine own self be true, . . . thou canst not then be false to any man." The Bard was a wee bit of a male chauvinist, of course, but mostly his Elizabethan insouciance was right on anyway!

But the trick is: *How* can we screw our heads on right? Must we needs deliver our brains to the neighborhood shrink to unscramble at forty dollars per hour? The answer, for almost all of us, is NO, DAMMIT, we can shape our *own* destiny. Having failed so brilliantly to improve the world, the time has come to devote some of our energies to *improving ourselves!* None of us is as effective, liberated, spontaneous, creative, and fulfilled as we could be—and have a right to try to be. Most of us are lonelier, more troubled, less alive, more anxious, and more throttled than we have to be. Is our fate writ in the stars or can we take ourselves by the scruff of the neck—of course it's late and we are scruffier than we should be, but better late than never—and shake ourselves truly alive?

Vorspan says: "Each person can take one's personality in hand, place it on the anvil of life and beat it into better shape." So beat it already!

Even *you?* Can *you* shape up?

Well, it's a challenge. You are rather a mess. Even your bad habits have sprouted bad habits. But even *you* can help yourself if you are willing to work at self-improvement. Honest. If you are content with your status quo (which can be described as the mess you are in), this book is not for you. Thomas Edison said: "Restlessness is discontent—and discontent is the first necessity of progress. Show me a thoroughly satisfied man and I will show you a failure." And he went out and unhappily invented the light bulb.

If you are dissatisfied with your life, if you want more out of it and more out of yourself, there is available a number of valuable guides to self-improvement. True, some of them promise too much . . . mental peace, spiritual power, liberation, serenity, potency, perfect faith (and perfect pitch?) . . . but some may be good for what ails you. In these pages we'll extract the pith of a dozen of the current self-help manuals, thus sparing you a hundred pith stops and—who knows?—perhaps getting you off the dime. We will try to help you appreciate yourself, to feel *OK,* to live with a neurotic without going bonkers, to be a winner instead of a loser, to be your own best friend, to smoke less and enjoy it a millimeter more, to be decisive and to stop phumphking so much, to kvetch less and enjoy it more, to discern the games people play, to cope with your aggressions, to translate body language into mama loshen, to practice TM, to stay awake when you are depressed and vice versa, to discount the BS factor, to put a tiger in your sexual tank, to melt your blubber in macrobiotic diet and to do a number on those who manipulate you. You ask us how we can promise so much? The answer is, don't ask. Read. Trust me, your cheerful guide. I am not altogether sure I understand everything I know about this stuff, but I'm OK, even though you are a pain in the neck.

Wittenstein, whoever he was, once described the philosopher's task as that of "showing the fly the way out of the flybottle." Christopher Morley once wrote: "When you sell a man a book, you don't sell him just twelve ounces of paper and ink and glue . . . you sell him a whole new life."

So buy this book already (though it weighs only eight ounces) and straighten up and fly right out of the bottle.

A.V.

Hillsdale, New York, 1976

# CONTENTS

## Chapter 1   I'M OK, THANKS TO TA

What's your bottom-line problem anyway? Is it that you don't quite feel *good* about yourself? Do you have the feeling that those around you are happy but that you have a permanent case of the blahs? Do you have a sense that others are operating on all their cylinders, but that you are sputtering along on maybe one and a half? Do you feel that you're growing *older,* but not really growing *up?*

OK, then, please step into the office and drop your fears. We may have just the right treatment for you. It is called Transactional Analysis; it is a technique for understanding our own mental processes; it doesn't hurt, and it might even help.

One of the most promising do-it-yourself guidebooks for understanding our own mental processes is the "transactional analysis." Dr. Eric Berne first conceived of the elements of the "transaction" and he put them to work in the book *Games People Play.* Later, Dr. Thomas A. Harris refined the ideas further in his *I'm OK, You're OK.* The heart of the Harris concept is that there are three real people—or, better, states of being—inside each of us. One is the small "Child" dominated by feelings. Another is the "Parent," a reflection of what each of us saw and heard his parents say or do when we were little. The third is the "Adult"—a logical, rational, grown-up, mature person. How these three stooges interact within us, varying with each "transaction" (encounter), defines our personality. This is the beauty part.

The Parent is the vast mishmash of recordings in the brain of external events perceived in one's first few years, primarily the first five. What our parents did and said is recorded in our Parent. For each of us the Parent recordings is different—a unique collection of rules and regulations, facial expressions of parents, including the looks of dismay (as when we painted the living room wall with Mom's lipstick) and the looks of delight (when we left home for college). The recorder was always on. It was never edited. It was like Nixon's White House, only it could not be erased. It lives in you as long as you live. It replays constantly, in stereo—two parents, maybe harmonizing, maybe clashing discordantly. Mostly, the Parent data is practical, life-giving, useful, sometimes very subtle; sometimes it is garbage ("Never wear your rubbers inside the house, you'll catch cold."). Lots of your later quirks, obsessions, and kinkiness, like your tendency to overheat in the car when the other lane moves faster than yours, stems from this stored Parent data. Look, nobody ever promised you life would be a Free Lunch.

The Child is, basically, the recording of INTERNAL happenings, the responses of the young lad or lass to what is seen and heard. Inasmuch as the little person had no real vocabulary during these tender years in which the most crucial of his experiences took place, he reacts with FEEL-

INGS. If Daddy skewered him with an angry look, he could not interpret this by recognizing that Daddy had a lousy day at the office, or Mommy was bugging Dad all through dinner. No, he reacts with FEELINGS. Like: WHAT DID I DO WRONG NOW? IT'S MY FAULT. Mostly, these feelings, as a result of the frustrating and civilizing process of being "raised," are negative, causing the little tyke to conclude early on: "I'M NOT OK." These feelings are recorded in the brain, stick there permanently like barnacles, and cannot be erased. Even the child of kind, loving parents inevitably develops the "I'M NOT OK" syndrome. It's built in and comes with the territory.

### Hook the Child

Once we grow up we still find ourselves in situations which "hook the child," bringing about a playback of the childish feelings of anger, rejection, jealousy, abandonment, frustration, etc. For example, I still cannot leave any food on my plate because of the starving Chinese. Thus Harris claims, "When a person is in the grip of feelings, we say his CHILD has taken over. When his anger dominates his reason, we say his CHILD is in command." So far, so bad. But, at the same time, there is also a vast reservoir of positive data in the CHILD . . . the warm feelings of first discovery, of glorious delights also carefully and permanently recorded. This is the flip side, the "I'M OK" side of the CHILD data. But, alas, the NOT OK overmatches the I'M OK. Thus, every person has a NOT OK CHILD bustling inside his brain, coloring his personality, cluttering his computer. By the time he enters kindergarten, he has twenty-five thousand hours of recordings whirring inside him, not to mention fifty thousand hours of TV stretching ahead of him.

As the little person gets older, he begins to self-actualize. He finds he can move around, manipulate objects, find things out for himself—things that are different from the "taught concept" of life in his PARENT and the "felt concept" of life in his CHILD. Beginning at the age of ten months, he begins to evolve a "thought concept" of life. This is the beginning of ADULT data. The embryonic ADULT, in the early years, can easily be deflected by commands from the PARENT and fear in the CHILD. Despite setbacks, the ADULT usually continues to develop more and more effectively as the maturation process continues. Later, the ADULT seeks to test the data in the PARENT, judging whether it is true and still worthwhile today, perhaps rejecting it; and examining the CHILD to determine whether the feelings there are appropriate to the current situation. Says Harris: "We cannot erase the recording, but we can choose to turn it off." However, best keep the ADULT plugged in, even when the CHILD is playing, or you'll never take yes for an answer.

### Free Up Your Adult

We grow up with four different possible combinations, depending on the interactions of PARENT, CHILD, and ADULT: I'M NOT OK—YOU'RE OK . . . I'M NOT OK —YOU'RE NOT OK . . . I'M OK—YOU'RE NOT OK . . . I'M OK—YOU'RE OK. Harris thinks the fourth is best. Well, OK, let's stay with him a while longer. Unfortunately, according to Harris, most people go through life in the "I'M NOT OK—YOU'RE OK" position, which is definitely not OK. One can lift himself from one position to another, but it's not easy. It takes a hell of a lot of operating ADULT to make the climb, because the ADULT has a hard time overtaking the PARENT and the CHILD. And if you don't have a freed-up ADULT, forget it.

Whatever our position, we play "games" which reflect our inner tapes. Games are described by Berne as "an ongoing series of complementary ulterior transactions progressing to a well-defined, predictable outcome. Descriptively, it is a recurring set of transactions, often repetitious, superficially plausible, with a concealed motivation or, more colloquially, a series of moves with a snare, or 'gimmick.'"

The object of Transactional Analysis is to give the patient real choice, freedom to change, the capacity to grow. Ideally, the patient learns the truth about what is in the PARENT and what is in the CHILD and how these things affect his current transactions. This should free up his ADULT, liberating him for truth, change, and freedom. God bless his ADULT.

A basic game, originating in childhood, is MINE IS BETTER THAN YOURS.

Like all other games, it is intended to offer a little relief from the distress of the I'M NOT OK position. Less common are the WHY DON'T YOU, YES BUT; the AIN'T IT AWFUL; IF IT WEREN'T FOR YOU, I COULD; LET'S YOU AND HIM FIGHT and NOW I'VE GOT YOU, YOU SON OF A BITCH. And don't think these games are funny. Not on your PAC. They are, all of them, defenses against the distress of feeling NOT OK.

Now, what has all this to do with YOU? It is not easy to see. Your PAC is a mess. Your recorder erased your first five years. You are suffering from a severe case of marasmus (which is a lack of stroking) and, although you had a strong PARENT, a lovely CHILD, and a spectacular ADULT, you remained such a bore that nobody wanted to transact with you. Hard as you try, you seem never to be able to stay in your ADULT, falling out sometimes under the most embarrassing circumstances, such as having a temper tantrum while in the dentist's chair. Some of your best friends won't tell you that you have a contaminated P, a blocked-up A, and a cockamamey C, leading to a duplex transaction of the most aggravated type. Now the whole neighborhood will go.

### Getting It On In Group

No, transactional analysis is not for you. You're permanently NOT OK. I, on the other hand, am definitely OK, thanks to the transactional groups I joined in Vallejo, California, which got my head screwed on just right. I remember it vividly . . .

LEADER: Ah, I see we have a new person with us. What's your name?

ME: Me Bernard.

LEADER: Have you paid your fee yet, Bernard?

ME: Yes, of course.

LEADER: I see. Were you irritated when I asked you about the fee?

ME: No, of course not. Why should I be irritated?

LEADER: Because your PARENT was playing back, Bernard. ALWAYS pay your money. Don't sneak in. AL-WAYS IS ALWAYS PARENT, Bernard. Sneaking in is CHILD. Getting irritated is also CHILD. *Feelings.* ADULT is rational understanding that anything you get for nothing is worth just that. I don't bring up the fee business because I'm interested in money, but only so you will value this experience. Do you understand?

ME: Not really, but I guess I'll pick it up as we go along.

LEADER: OK, Bernard, you're OK. Now, who else would like to analyze the transaction between me and Bernard up to this point? Somebody?

SOMEBODY: I will. Bernard came in here with his CHILD hanging out. It must have been like his first day at kindergarten—new faces, new people, new challenges. Wetting his pants. Fear. Anxiety. And when you spoke, his PARENT cut in, laying on him rules, regulations, proprieties, the whole trip. And you, of course, were ADULT in asking him about the fee right away.

LEADER: You think I was testing him?

SOMEBODY: No, you were being practical, as always. You know goddam well what a crock this PAC stuff is and the only reason you do it is to rip off the Yo-yo before he finds out.

LEADER: Ah, so. Now you are playing AIN'T IT AWFUL with me, aren't you?

SOMEBODY: Up your contaminated ADULT with your blocked-out PARENT!

LEADER: You see, Bernard? We are free here to express ourselves, to get in touch with our real feelings, to express feelings—however negative—without regard to race, color, sex, or previous condition of servitude. Now, let us get to your problem, which is what again?

BERNARD: I am a defrocked priest for the FBI.

LEADER: I see. And?

BERNARD: My job was to infiltrate the Berrigans and the Catholic revolutionary movements.

LEADER: I see. And what is the problem?

BERNARD: I got caught blowing up a draft board, everybody else ran away, and the judge put me in the slammer for six years.

LEADER: But if you worked for the FBI . . .

BERNARD: They said that they couldn't blow my cover and I could help my country by intercepting Berrigan's mail, putting LSD in his tuna, and bugging his cell.

LEADER: And did you?

BERNARD: Yes, but then the CIA recruited me, offering me a private cell and an expense account, explaining to me that the FBI is a commie front.

LEADER: Oh, wow!

BERNARD: The bottom line is that I developed a bad case of command impotence.

LEADER: Of course. You were screwed by too many NOT OK government agencies. Now let's just separate out your P, A, and C and see if we can stand you up again . . .

## A Case History

Actually, thanks to PAC transactional analysis, I have been able to fire my shrink, whose office was decorated in overwrought furniture. Now I am capable of analyzing myself. Let me give you an example. Just the other day a scowling black stranger approached me in Times Square. He looked rather seedy and frightening.

STRANGER: Gimme a match.

I (to myself): Oh, oh, I'm gonna be mugged. I'd better activate my PAC pronto.

MY PARENT: I don't carry matches, could start a fire. I don't smoke, bad for one's health.

MY CHILD: I'm not OK. I'm scared shitless. This dude's gonna cream me. Ahhhhh!

MY ADULT: Don't be foolish. It's broad daylight. The street is full of people. The man merely wants a match, for gosh sake, don't make such a scene! Just because he's black doesn't mean he's a mugger. Don't be a bigot. You're OK!

I: No match, sorry. It's a slow season.

STRANGER: Gimme your money.

MY PARENT: I don't carry money, could lose it.

MY CHILD: Oh, oh, he'll break my bones. WHY ME? Who did I ever hurt? I'm gonna cry!

MY ADULT: Just explain him, shmuck! You're *OK!*

I (murmuring): No money.

STRANGER: No match, no money, not OK. I'm gonna have to break you in two.

PARENT: Never talk to strangers. Why don't you stay in your ADULT?

CHILD: Scream! This sonofabitch is *not OK,* even if he *is* black. I'm not OK, the whole scene is *not OK.*

ADULT: Explain him you're a member of the NAACP!

I: . . . tell me, do you accept credit cards?

STRANGER: Surely, but it will take just a moment to check your credit rating.

PAC WINS AGAIN!

One caveat: Some people have blocked-out PARENTS. This is bad news. Harris tells us that experiments have been conducted with monkeys who were brought up not by their real mommies, but by substitute mothers in the form of wire dummies covered with terry cloth. In infancy, these little monkeys became warmly attached to their surrogate terry-cloth mommies. However, when they matured, their ability to reproduce and rear their own young monkeys was minimal, to say the least. Mothering was simply not recorded in their PARENT, so there was no appropriate playback. So if, by any chance, your mother was a terry-cloth wire dummy, don't monkey around with the rest of this book. It will make you go ape. So go read *Be the Person You Were Meant to Be.*

## *Chapter II*   **BECOMING THE MENSCH YOU WERE MEANT TO BE**

Do you go around like a psychic Typhoid Mary, poisoning the wells of your own personality and lousing up your relationships with others? Do you suffer from foot-in-mouth disease? Do you let the negative effects of *past* experiences pollute the potentialities of the *present?* Do you have that sick feeling that somehow you have never emerged as the person you were *meant* to be? Do you get your back up when people bug you with dumb questions like these?

Shame!

There is a sure-fire way to instant salvation! You don't need a shrink, a PAC computer, an encounter group, or anything else. All you need is Dr. Jerry Greenwald, whose book, *Be the Person You Were Meant to Be,* teaches you how to determine whether your behavior is emotionally *nourishing* or emotionally *toxic*. Once you have mastered this tool, there is no need for digging into the rabbit warrens of your forgettable past, no costly treatments, no exotic therapy. You can rebuild your life with your own hands. Greenwald offers you a handy mirror to see how you look to others. He gives you a dramatically powerful way of revamping your entire life-style and becoming "A WHOLE NEW YOU."

Knowing you, it couldn't happen a minute too soon!

*Be the Person You Were Meant to Be* is based on Gestalt psychology. This holds that you don't have to dig into your past, because you will probably only stir up a lot of dirt and dust, reinforcing the destructive effects of obsolete experiences. No, we can get rid of the *toxic* effects of these past experiences and behavior patterns by latching on to the present. Dr. Greenwald's book is aimed at lessening our unnatural (*toxic*) behavior in getting along with ourselves and others, while stressing the discovery of natural (*nourishing*) attitudes and ways of behaving. As Greenwald puts it: "The goal of Gestalt therapy is to melt the *toxic* power of the past by learning to focus on the present." Leaving aside the obvious question as to what's so peachy keen about the present—and the future is also a can of worms—let us follow the doctor's analysis, which, deep down, may be shallow but, nonetheless, rewarding, especially to him.

Each of us is a mixture of T (*Toxic*) qualities and N (*Nourishing*) qualities. T qualities include putting down people, manipulating others, being overcritical, taking our cues from others (like our parents) rather than our own desires and interests, seeing life as hostile or meaningless, focusing on the negative, conforming, punishing one's self, inflicting guilt. N qualities include spontaneity, autonomy, unashamed self-concern, the capacity for intimacy, building people up instead of tearing them down, taking risks of reaching out for what one wants, self-acceptance, flexibility, letting it all hang out. If our T characteristics predominate, we are T people, even if we never enter a T group. If our N qualities predominate, we are N people. If you want to know which YOU are, listen to yourself when you and your spouse leave a party. If you poor-mouth the food, the company, the house, the conversation, and the games (Hump the Hostess is passé), you're a T person who drips poison wherever you go.

You can also measure yourself by your clothes. If you are 1000 per cent N, you'll weave and make your own garments. If the neighbors don't like your purple loincloth or your pink sarong, they're T people and the hell with them anyway. If, on the other hand, you go to the department store, which everyone tells you is THE place to buy your clothes, and you let the salesman with the Smith Brothers beard intimidate you into buying what HE likes, you're very much T and your clothes will reflect your individual identity much less than they will reflect the ephemeral style of the moment.

Dr. Greenwald gives us many check lists by which we can grade ourselves in terms of N and T. Here are a few sample questions:

Nourishing: Do I decide what's most important for me?

or

Toxic: Do I allow others to make decisions for me?

Nourishing: Do I take responsibility for satisfying my own needs?

or

Toxic: Do I try to manipulate other people into doing it for me?

Nourishing: Do I see life as exciting and stimulating?

or

Toxic: Do I experience myself struggling to stay alive in a jungle of hostile forces?

Nourishing: Do I accept my mistakes as an inevitable part of learning?

or

Toxic: When I do something that displeases me, do I attack myself with ridicule, disgust, or self-punishment?

If you got four Ns, you can skip the rest of this chapter, because you're already too healthy to bear. If you got four Ts, you'll only poor-mouth the book and the author, which I am too T to cope with.

### Getting from T to N

But if we are model T types and go around poisoning the wells of our own personality and our relationships with others, what can we *do* about it? We could slash our wrists or put our heads in the oven, but that is obviously the T way out. What must needs be done is to cultivate antidotes against the T poisons in our makeup! If we suffer from "approvalitis"—definitely a T bone in your throat—how can we conquer it? If we are prone to "appreciationitis"—in which we feel compelled constantly to do things for others so they will "appreciate" us—how do we get off the stick? If we are subject to "explanationitis"—the constant need to explain and defend oneself to others—is there any way to be cured? And what if we're afflicted with "nice-guyitis"? Is that as bad as phlebitis? Or "personal performeritis," in which we constantly compare ourselves with ourselves, especially in sexual acrobatics? "Emotional constipation"? "Psychological diarrhea"? How do we get from T to N?

The answer: Self-awareness. The key to self-awareness?
you guessed it—Dr. Jerry Greenwald's *Be the Person You
Were Meant to Be*. Although it is admittedly a slim volume,
it is nonetheless soporific.

After intensive self-analysis, the author has been able to
figure out the persons he was meant to be . . .

| | |
|---|---|
| Wilbur Mills | Mae West |
| Margaret Sanger | Diamond Jim Brady |
| Judas Iscariot | Thomas Paine |
| Archibald Cox | Henry VII |
| Marie Dionne | Wayne Terwilliger |
| Peter the Great | Thomas Best |
| Nasser | Sarah Bernhardt |
| Ben-Hur | Sihanouk |
| Golda Meir | Evel Knievel |
| Adlai Stevenson | Potiphar |
| Marie Dressler | Philo |
| Florence Nightingale | Pluto |
| Harold Ickes | Peter Pan |

Personally, I don't think the best way to categorize people is on the basis of their N or T. It doesn't fit well. For example, a friend of mine is a Dashing Dan commuter on the
Long Island Railroad. He doesn't leave the house in the
morning until the train actually passes his house. Then he
shouts at his wife to start the car, roars into the car, slopping his coffee on his New York *Times* and his briefcase,
and they race the train to the station. What's his behavior,
aside from being lunatic?

The frenzy is *toxic,* the coffee is *nourishing,* and he and
his wife have a moment of family togetherness. Once he

boards the train, he has an elaborate ritual (which includes hiding in the men's room) to avoid running into any friend, relative, or acquaintance so he can bury his head in the *Times* undisturbed. How can we characterize his behavior? Toxic? Nourishing? I'm afraid neither category applies because the author's basic premise is wrong. The great Samuel Pepys once watched two women arguing across a back fence. "They will never agree," he said. "They are arguing from different premises." Pepys had moxie and he was damn straight, the person he was *meant* to be!

### TTs and Ls

I think Greenwald's division is not the only—or most—crucial way to divide human beings. There are two categories of people—those who categorize and those who don't. In my categorizing, the most important is the division between Talk-Talkers and Listeners. Talk-Talkers are those who seem to feel that they can talk their way to a truth that they didn't even know they possessed. They are usually regarded as bores, however bright they are. I know an L who was taken to lunch by a TT (TTs usually pick up the tab; Ls are too busy listening to notice the check). TT talked from Bloody Mary to coffee; L never opened his mouth. After lunch, TT felt so nourished that he told L, "You know, you're the brightest lawyer I ever met." (L is a tax accountant; while appearing to listen, he is inventing tax shelters in his head.) Ls, naturally, are always asked to be confidantes for other people's troubles and are always asked to give personal advice, which they never do—and that is a good thing —because their private lives are disasters, their spouses complaining, "You never tell me anything." Successful shrinks are always Ls in the office and TTs at home. Good listeners always can sit by the hour, looking intent and deeply empathetic, having been born with the faculty of sleeping with their eyes wide open and NEVER falling off the chair.

A good example of the difference between a TT and a GL (Good Listener) is Mohammed Ali and Joe Louis. Louis never talked in the ring; rarely out of it. Flamboyant Ali tried to blow out his "bums" with his mouth as well as his fists. Louis never had to rush around yelling, "I am the greatest." Everybody knew it, including Max Schmeling, who was a TT until the second Louis fight—and a GL ever after!

TTs feel they have to do all the talking because they like good conversation.

Nobody can be a TT without relying on an arsenal of cliches. Every TT is a cliche artist. Lyndon Johnson and Richard Nixon were among our greatest run-off-at-the-mouth Presidents. The former nailed our "coonskin" to the wall in Vietnam and the latter gave us the joys of Watergate and its ineffable tapes, affording us a rare opportunity to hear exactly how a titanic TT talks (while the Ship of State sinks). Listening to the "big enchilada" and his crew of fast-talking lackeys on their lamented tapes was, disgust and shame aside, a revealing treat, instead of a treatment, of the shallowest string of cliches to which the English language can be subjected. They trotted out "scenarios," which will "never play in Peoria," putting a "cap on the lid," "screwing our enemies," letting friends "twist slowly in the wind," starting "whole new ballgames," "pulling the plugs," "offering an hors d'oeuvre," "hunkering down," knowing where the "bodies are buried," "playing it by ear," "at this point in time," etc., etc. If Nixon and his cohorts had been GLs, instead of TTs, he'd still be contaminating the White House and they would have stayed out of the slammer. So shut up a while. Silence is golden (although, Harry Golden never buttoned his lip).

Even TTs can't talk all the time; sometimes they pause for breath. TTs are very poor listeners, because they fancy themselves as the center of the universe and everyone else as minor planets, orbiting around *them*. Example: a TT's secretary comes into the office, weeping.

TT: What's wrong?

SECRETARY: My mother died in Denver.

TT: Denver? Oh, I once had an account in Denver!

TTs tend to become clergymen, commentators, government flaks, barbers, teachers, newspapermen, lawyers, politicians, gamblers, waiters, advertising copy writers and secretaries of state. Ls tend toward lucrative careers in psychiatry, jockeys, surveillance, plumbing, and crime, and they excel in chess.

Another vital division is between the Night People and the Day People. Night people simply function best at night, reading or roaming the neighborhood or listening to the radio talk shows until dawn. Night people fade in the daylight, either going to sleep—hibernation—or running out of gas before coffee-break time at the office. Day people are the opposite—full of more bounce to the ounce all day, but running down like an unwound clock in the evening. The research of Soyer, Fergassen, and Krock suggests that there is a positive correlation between T (Talkers) and NP (Night People), but the follow-up study of Hermione

Shmedbeck says these samplings were skewed. Shmedbeck posits the hypothesis that Ls talk in their sleep more than Ts —she calls this the nocturnal redress syndrome.

You can figure out where you belong by honestly answering the following question:

What would you do if:

You came home in the middle of the day and found your mate in bed with your best friend.

Options:

1. Pretend you saw nothing.
2. Beat up your mate.
3. Beat up your best friend.
4. Beat both.
5. Demand an explanation.
6. Pack.
7. Make them promise not to do it again.
8. Say to your best friend: "Look, I *have* to, but you?"

## *Chapter III* **STUDY BODY LANGUAGE**

When we travel to a foreign country without knowledge of the language of the land, we can have a good time, sure. But naked to the tongue we are perforce strangers, onlookers, outlanders. We can tiptoe through the tulips, or haggle at the bazaar, photograph everything, and buy every item that's not nailed down. But—still—it's like taking a bath in your underwear. It's not the genuine article. Familiarity with the language is the open sesame, the true rite of passage, the golden door. Knowing the language is *in-house;* ignorance is *out-house* (and in the war against ignorance, you are a conscientious objector). Even a smattering of vocabulary, uttered laboriously as if the words will break your teeth, sets you off from the wide-eyed throngs being handed sheeplike from one tourist guide to the next.

Body language is the true universal Esperanto. Even if you don't know a "shmetterlink" from an "andiamo," you can learn to read the meaning of a shrug, a rotating foot, a dilated nostril, an eye contact, or a vibrating gonad, and your sensitivity to people will sharpen even if you don't understand a word they say. You will learn to *read* people, even if what they are saying is *Greek* to you. You will be more fully human, more acutely aware, more open to the nuances of the human condition.

For we send signals to each other, even when we don't exchange a word. In Julius Fast's book, *Body Language* (Human Potential Paperback), we learn that the body telegraphs our thoughts. The science of Kinesics explains the physical messages we flash in the ways we cross our legs, carry our shoulders, fold our arms, sit, stand, walk, and move our eyes and mouth. Through body language we signal our perceptions of ourselves and of others. Show Fast where a person sits when entering a room full of people, and how he or she settles into a chair, and he can tell you if that person is a leader, a toucher, a heavy vocalizer (big mouth), shy, lonely, or aggressive. Nonverbal communication is as revealing—and maybe less masking—than verbal communication.

For example, Fast describes an unsettling luncheon date he had with a good friend. They sat opposite each other in a restaurant. Silently the friend placed his cigarettes down on his side of the table; but, as the conversation developed, he silently moved his cigarettes in a few small movements to Dr. Fast's side of the table. Fast couldn't understand why he felt mildly distressed until the friend explained that he had, deliberately, experimented with the movement of his property (cigarettes) into Fast's unspoken "territorial zone." Unconsciously, this was perceived as an act of aggression by Fast. The same thing happens when an automobile driver cuts us off, invading our "space" or our "turf." How come we get so furious and go honking and cursing down the highway after the offender? Why so much frenzy? Dr. Fast tells us why.

Or take the story of Aunt Grace. She had become old

and a little senile. A debate raged through the family as to whether or not she should be placed in a home for the aged. Aunt Grace seemed very cool about it, insisting that she was quite prepared to do whatever the family thought best. Meanwhile, she sat in the midst of the family discussions, caressing her necklace and running one hand along the velvet of the couch, then feeling a wood carving. Finally the family read the message. Aunt Grace was telling them, silently but eloquently, via body language, that she was lonely and hungry for companionship and tender loving care, and needing help. Like Aunt Grace, each of us is transmitting messages to the outside world. Especially my friend Jacques, who is the champion long-distance, dried-manure thrower in Québec (130 feet).

Fast argues that many of our body language signals are more subtle than Aunt Grace's. We cross our arms; we shrug our shoulders; we wink; we stare; we slap our foreheads; we drum our fingers impatiently on the desk; we tap our feet; we scratch our noses; we cross our legs; we protrude our boobs. Whether consciously or unconsciously, we are saying something in each of these gestures. We are what we feel, and our body gestures convey our inner feelings. You know, I'm sure, what this is a lot of.

My research tends to confirm Fast's theories, but I also found that the kind of car we drive is equally revealing of our inner thoughts. The man who drives a powerful gas-guzzler may well be sublimating his own fears of lack of potency. If he can get it up to seventy miles an hour in twelve seconds, he definitely can get it up. On the other hand, small folk who drive Volkswagen beetles obviously wish, as they twist in the fetal position, to return to the womb.

Are these body signals instinctive? Are they universal, regardless of culture? Do people smile when they are happy, frown when upset, stare in hate in all cultures and societies? Fast believes so. I don't. Research on the Mog Mog natives of Ulithi island in the Carolines calls Fast's conclusions into doubt. There, researchers found, the natives smiled when they stubbed their toes, cried when they were tickled, laughed when pickled, frowned when they made love, stared when they ate and watched television in the middle of the night. Were they mutated or what? Who knows? Let's hear it for Mog Mog!

### The Party

Let us now take the insights we have learned from Fast and apply them to a real-life American situation. The party is about to begin. The hostess is asking her husband how come there is no bourbon and no tonic water—does she have to think of everything?—all the while pushing under the beds mountains of clothes, books, and records that she does not have the time to put away. The doorbell rings. The hostess grits her teeth, stomps on the floor, and thrusts the index finger of her right hand into the air. We know from our reading that she is sending the following message: "WHICH OF THOSE GODDAM *MOTHERS* IS ACTUALLY ARRIVING AT THE TIME I INVITED THEM TO ARRIVE!" Silently kicking her husband's shin (meaning: "I get a kick out of you") she goes to the door, pasting a masklike smile on her face, and lets the first couple in, Hank and Susie Dreck.

Hank's face looks furrowed and quizzical (translation:

"Oh, Christ, why did we have to be the first to come, since I plan to be the first to *leave*"), while Sue's face is marked by a raised eyebrow ("If her house looks like the wreck of the Hesperus *now*, when she's having *company*, what does it look like *normally?*") and a radiant smile ("Anyway the bar is set up"). Hank winks at his host (saying, "The game is in extra innings, where the hell is your TV set?"). The host shrugs his shoulders (*"I'm* not going to turn it on; she'll drive a stake through my heart on the spot. *You* turn it on, then I'll watch with you, I should be rude to my company?").

The second couple enters. He is Alex, a tiny almost invisible man; she is Jane, a tall strapping Amazon. Alex proceeds to walk *UNDER* the rug. We know from our studies that he is really saying, "I am nothing; I do not exist." Jane strides across the room, crunching him like a bug in the rug as she goes (meaning: "Look who is trying to be a nothing"). She finally stops at midpoint, stretches her legs apart, caresses her slinking hips, tosses her mane and whinnies. From our studies, we know that Jane is a true thoroughbred, a natural leader and a member of the horsy set. By her gestures, she is really saying, "Win, place, or show, I am a somebody. Me Jane."

Actually, I don't know all that much from Body English. In fact, ever since I went to an ulpan to learn Hebrew, my body has forgotten English (it tells me I am no WASP, I am a WASH—White Anglo-Saxon Hebrew) and it speaks from right to left. However, being a person who has survived some 13,747 meetings of various committees over the past twenty-five years, I *have* become a mavin on the particular type of body language which speaks so eloquently when people gather about a table to have a meeting. Here are some of the stigmata which Julius *Fast* seems very *slow* in picking up:

## Meetings

The chairman is about to open the meeting. He looks at his watch. His eyebrows rise (which says, "Oy, it's already eight thirty, I'd like to get out of here in time for Howard Cosell's second half"). He calls the meeting to order and asks Millie Gefarelick if she would read the minutes of the last meeting.

Millie says all right and stands up with a weak smile and plows into the minutes, the smile never leaving her face, even while she describes the get-well messages and condolences sent to an assortment of failing and already failed members of the group. (The half smile says: "If they ever do a number on me to make me be secretary again, I'll give these sexists a rejection they can't refuse. Why me? Why not one of these male rinky-dinks who never lift a finger for the club?")

Sam Enderly came in late, his eyes jerking quickly ("Where can I sit down near an *exit?*"), and bowed gracefully to Millie (the better to look down her dress) and settled into his seat, crossing his left leg over his right (meaning: "So my foot won't fall asleep before I do").

The chairman then called on Sidney Gelt to give the treasurer's report. While Gelt droned through his numbers, the chairman patted his ample paunch (meaning: "Already I've had a belly full of Gelt") and twitched his knee ("liberal knee-jerk reaction").

It was now time for the calling of cards and the raising of

funds. Body language became thunderous. Many members rolled their eyes. Everybody squirmed in his seat. Sam woke up with a start (meaning: "Let's put a stop to this"). Dr. Jason had that down-in-the-mouth look ("I'm a dentist"). One man nervously combed his hair ("hair-raising experience") as the professional fund-raiser calmly tied each victim's shoelaces together and nailed his shoes to the floor. One wealthy man slid his wallet into his wife's purse, knowing that he would soon be turned upside down so that all his money would be shaken out of him. And, of course, one dowager slapped her forehead loudly (meaning: "But I'm not even a member here; isn't this the Weight Watchers?"). While all these antics were going on, the professional fund-raiser smiled with his eyes ("Go on, wiggle, the moment of truth is approaching; I'll cut you off at the pass"), did a little veronica ("Olé, it's kill-time") and then wiped them all out with his coup de grâce, earning for his efforts two ears, a tail, and some $774.29 *new money.*

### Subway

There is also a very special body English for riding the subway, elbows akimbo, eyes down (so you won't trip over bodies or catch the eye of a mugger), and—for women—both hands on your purse (the better to reach the hatpin and the spray can if need be). When bodies are pressed together in the rush-hour crush, drape your newspaper over your body to protect yourself from lawsuit and/or rape. In entering the subway door—only half of which, by New York tradition, ever opens—proceed briefcase first because the door is trained to slam on your wrist. When standing in a swaying car, get your hand on a strap, a pole, or an Italian; if this is not possible, stand on the balls of your feet and rock gently. Do not let yourself stand flat-footed because a short stop can scatter you all over Chelsea, and it is harder to bail out. Also, talk to yourself—at least move your lips. Otherwise, you will look *suspicious*, like a suburbanite *walking* to the corner store when he should be *driving his car*.

Some New Yorkers have an excess of body language on the subway. For example, there is the crew that stands first on one foot, then on the other, on the Penn Station uptown express platform in the morning rush hour, peering down the tunnel to see whether the local or express is emerging first. If it is the express, their face muscles relax and they rock back and forth on their toes. If nothing is coming, their feet paw the platform like bison at bay and they snort a lot. If the local appears, they put their heads down, raise their right hands, and shout "Banzai" and stampede in a thundering herd down the stairs, through the concourse, and up the down stairs of the local, hurling themselves huffing and puffing into the open half-door. It is good fun, it saves thirty seconds and it is the only exercise these New Yorkers ever get, unless they are CIA men testing nerve gases on the IRT.

When body language is misread, it can cause much mischief. Recently, an elderly and devout Jew gave his children fits. They thought he had converted to Christianity because he seemed to cross himself every time he left the house.

"Nonsense," he said, when they confronted him. "I touch my right side to make sure I have my glasses and my left to be sure I have my handkerchief. I put my hand up to my head to make sure my yarmulke is on, and I touch my fly to make sure it's buttoned."

*Chapter IV*  **BECOMING YOUR OWN
BEST FRIEND**

Is part of your *angst* that you tend to look to others—instead of yourself—for self-esteem and self-acceptance? Do you go around with an invisible marquee over your head that lights up: *"FEED ME"*? Do you know how to run your automobile better than you know how to run *yourself*? Are you hung up that others will think you are "selfish" if you look after your *own* needs and satisfactions? If the answer is none of the above, skip to Chapter V. If the answers to the above are all YES, you need a strong pill of self-awareness which you can have, nicely sugar-coated, in *How to Be Your Own Best Friend*.

This little do-it-yourself book, written by Newman and Berkowitz—two psychiatrists who are married to each other —is a remarkable work. In simple English, avoiding jargon and the lumpy language of the trade, the authors tell us how to be our own best friend, which is nice when one considers that a friend is a gift we give to ourselves. They tell us how to *use* time rather than "killing it," and they quote the late Bernard Berenson who, at the age of ninety, wished he could stand at the side of the road and ask passers-by to drop off their "unused minutes." The authors urge us toward growth and change, encouraging us to take risks for fulfillment and happiness. Without poor-mouthing the psychiatric couch (they note they don't need a couch in their practice and have analyzed patients by telephone), they stress that most of us can *change* our lives through *self-awareness* and *self-acceptance*.

For example, they tell us not to be ashamed to be *selfish,* because we cannot love anyone else unless we love ourselves. The Bible admonishes us to love our neighbor "as ourselves," not "more than" ourselves.

Similarly, they note that most of us have patterns of thought and behavior which are self-defeating; with effort, we can track these patterns and *modify* them. We tend to look to others for recognition and esteem—we walk around with that look on our faces which says, "Feed me"—but the most meaningful compliment we can get is from *ourselves.* If our parents fouled us up a long time ago, we make matters worse by digging up the roots and heaping bitterness on them and self-pity on ourselves. Cut your losses; let the past bury the past; get on with the task of *living* with zest and joy. Don't blame everyone else; the solution lies within each of us, if we are only aware and honest enough to be part of the *solution* instead of the *problem.*

Simple common sense (and superb promotion) catapulted this slim volume into the best-seller list. But what is most intriguing is the format. An interviewer asks the doctors good questions; they give their unpretentious answers. But the responses of the two doctors are apparently so harmonious that they are "blended" in the book into one answer to each question. Not every shrinking husband-and-wife team is so compatible that they can be thus osterized.

In evaluating the Berkowitz-Newman technique, we duplicated the scene by going over the same ground with our own husband-and-wife team consisting of Dr. Morris Yennavelt and Dr. Wendy Farblundget, both of Los Angeles. Here is the unedited transcript of our taped conversation.

### The Tapes

INTERVIEWER: OK, let's just start from the top. I'll throw out the question and either one of you who wants to field it just step in and knock it out of the park. If the other wants to add something, that's super. Here's my first question: IS IT POSSIBLE FOR AN ORDINARY PERSON TO LEARN THE ART OF LIVING? I MEAN, ONE CAN LEARN HOW TO DANCE OR OPERATE A CAR, BUT CAN ONE LEARN HOW TO *ENJOY* ONE'S LIFE, TO BE HIS OWN *BEST FRIEND?*

MORRIS: Of course one can. If one buys our little book, which I hope you will hurry up and edit because pub date is in March—we had better beat Dr. Vasochvus to the bookstores—there is no doubt that it will provide the needed roadmap to self-appreciation and self-acceptance. I like to say that if you don't know where you are going, any route will get you there . . .

WENDY (interrupting): You certainly do like to say that, whether it applies or not. The simple answer to your banal question is the following: It depends. If a person comes to *own* his *own* life, yes. If a person continues to believe that real living is something she . . .

M: . . . or *he.*

W: Stop with that sexist chozerei already! . . . or *he* will be permitted to do sometime in the future, no. In either case, our little book wouldn't hurt.

I: But, look, you're both practicing analysts. Why should a person go to you for private therapy—at, say, $40 a fifty-minute hour—if he/she can get his/her head straightened out just reading our little book?

W: Nobody should read this little book INSTEAD of private therapy with a skilled talking head. Either *before* or *after,* fine. Not *instead*. This is not either/or; it is both/and. You want to get us stoned by the APA?

M: And we never said that a person had to READ our little book. That would be arrogant. We'd like them to BUY it; we really don't care whether they *read* it or not.

I: I see. Well, can you honestly say that most people you treat are happier after treatment than before they enter your office?

M: Yes, they ARE happier after they stop seeing me. Definitely. Most of them are such miserable bastards, you wouldn't believe. Sometimes I have to turn them over to the bill collectors, they're such a bunch of deadbeats, they should hang from their thumbs. Of course, the money doesn't mean all that much to me, but it does indicate a genuine disorder in the patient.

W: What a crock! Money is the only thing that DOES mean anything to you! When that zoftig young patient of yours disrobed and offered her body to you in lieu of payment, you told her, "OK, I'll feed you but you must feed me, too, your major medical pays it anyway." So don't give us this . . .

M: Why must you interrupt all the time? I don't interrupt

you, despite the fact that you are the weirdest witch doctor in all of LA . . .

W: You open your fat pisk one more time, I'll give you such a shot in the head you'll think it was Madam Zoftig's truck driver husband visiting you again . . .

M: You have no right to expose the details of my private practice. Did I tell this flake interviewer about the time you tried to exorcise the dybbuk from the minister's wife and she freaked out and ran back to the church and smashed up his organ?

I: Calm down, doctors, please. Let's remember what we're doing here. I'll have to edit those outbursts out of the tape. Now, let us proceed with a little more decorum, shall we? I want to put this question: Why is it that, despite the rapid growth of psychological knowledge and treatment, people seem to be less happy than ever? And, despite the rise in marriage counseling, our divorce rate is going right through the roof?

W: In the first place, marriage is a ridiculous institution and most people do not want to live in an institution. Secondly, the more one understands about himself and his partner—really UNDERSTANDS—the more impossible the marriage becomes. The healthy ones are the ones who split; and they are usually better friends *after* the divorce. It's the fearful, rigid, conforming personalities who feel that, having made their bed, they must sleep in it, but preferably in twin beds, separate bedrooms, or open marriages.

M: My wife is talking through her hat once again. Actually, the zooming divorce rate is culturally determined. In most societies, it is nothing like ours. We Americans have this dumb obsession with happiness, with love, with sexual ecstasy, with the veneration of youth. It's no wonder most people split in such a society. If we lived in a place like Tahiti, for example . . .

w: You'd be ripping off the natives for whatever the traffic would bear . . .

m: I'd be living out my fantasy with a young bare-breasted savage in a bamboo hut . . .

w: . . . and I would cut off your ear because I'm sick to death of your kvetching . . .

i (jumping up and down): WAIT A MINUTE! WAIT A MINUTE! Who will possibly want to read your slim volume about human relationships if they learn that you two hate each other's guts and can't get along even for half an hour? I mean, why do you two stay together anyway?

w: Believe it or not, we are very compatible. We both like to be savaged, punished, and abused. We both like to heap pain on the other. We are sickies, like everybody else. Nobody's perfect.

m: It also is better for us to file a joint return. We feed each other. We meet each other's basic needs. We are best friends to each other, second only to ourselves. That may not fulfill the all-American stereotype of marriage, but it is very functional. It works. What's your next question?

i: But how can you give advice to *others* then?

m: Watch what we do, not what we say. When the going gets tough, the tough get going.

w: Right on, Morris. When a new cliche is invented, Morris will steal it and call it *research*. His head is so full of garbage that, in a garbage-filled society like this one, he sounds wise as Solomon. His patients think he's the true

Messiah and psychiatry is the process of giving people what they want, not what they need. You understand?

I: OK, OK. Let's turn to child-rearing. Do you favor the permissive approach or do you think we must now tilt in the direction of greater discipline?

M: We're against child-rearing. Nobody should be responsible for another human being in such a world. We're for free vasectomies, abortion on demand, or, if necessary, infanticide.

I: Wow! That's quite severe, isn't it?

W: No, we don't think so. The central influence on a child's maturing mind in our culture is the Television. The average American family invests forty-two hours a week in television. Garbage in and garbage out. Turns the human brain into mashed potatoes. Did you ever watch *All in the Family?* Such drek. Gives bigotry a bad name. The only way to beat that monster is to deprive him of his future victims. Zero Population is the only answer.

I: Then what about posterity?

M: Who gives a bleep about posterity? What did posterity ever do for me or you? Does posterity have to live under a Lyndon Johnson, Dick Nixon, or Gerry Ford? Does posterity protect us against our violent patients?

I: Well, I'm not sure where we're going in this little chat, really. It's going to take a lot of editing. Well, let me try a different tack. Do either of you feel that a person can *learn* to be a loving, caring person? Is that a born instinct or an art to be cultivated?

W: You can learn how to *love.* You can learn how to *smile.* You can learn not to judge yourself too harshly. You can learn to dress to please *yourself.* You can learn to love *yourself,* your mate, and you can learn to love your own *parents.*

I: Good. But how?

W: Beats me. OK, Big Mouth, you tell him how.

M: By meditating. Silence is the way. Recite a mantra, count beads, stretch your spirit and get in tune with yourself, and the world will be filled with the spirit of love.

I: Do you follow that regimen yourself, doctor?

W: Big Mouth hasn't reduced his mouth traffic in forty years . . .

M: Listen, you fat slob, pipe down or I'll fall on you!

W: You don't know what you think. You're so open-minded your brains are falling out!

M: Madam, if you didn't have me as your seeing-eye dog through life, you'd long since have rotted away at the bottom of an open manhole!

I: Stop it, already, or I'll turn off the machine! Doctors, what brought you to my attention was your newly published research on the Yennavelt-Farblundget "ego vulnerability" test for measuring the strength of a person's self-identity. Would you tell us about the EV?

*EV Test*

W: What's with this *us* bit? I only see you and your crummy tape recorder. It's an old model, I hope it works.

M: Let me explain you. It's my turn. You told last time, Wendy, at the press conference. It's only fair.

W: OK, OK, but you'll gum it up. Go right to the point.

M: Well, our research has been hailed as a major breakthrough and a seminal conceptualization, utilizing a psychodramatic technique, simulating a verbal Rorschach or TAT test, patterned on . . .

w: Holy mackerel! Stop spouting the jargon we laid on the APA convention. This is supposed to be for the average American—a dumb, gum-chewing slob. Here's the trick! We conducted extensive interviews with each person in our sample, asking this and that, blah, blah, and then with no change of tone we ask the kicker: "Tell me, *what's really going to be with you?*" That's the whole ticket.

i: And what happens?

m: What happens is simple *murder.* You wouldn't *believe.* That question wipes out 93 per cent of the people we interview. It strips them of all defenses, exposes the frailty of their self-image, and brings out all their fears and self-doubts about who they are and where they are going. Most egos are so weak they have to be glued together with self-deception.

i: You mean that even successful persons—doctors, lawyers, college presidents, good parents, etc.—break down on that question?

m: Especially college presidents. Approximately 40 per cent of college presidents start weeping as if the Mau Maus had taken over their administration buildings again.

w: . . . yes, more men than women, too.

m: . . . and some 15 per cent become silently catatonic, 10 per cent sweat profusely, 5 per cent begin to shake, another 10 per cent break off the interview, and about 5 per cent go for our groin!

i: You said 93 per cent fall apart at this question. What about the other 7 per cent? Who are they and what gives them such ego strength?

M: Half of them are hard of hearing and the other half are revolting kids who know exactly what they are doing—collecting ten bucks for the dopey interview—and where they are going . . . back to the commune to regale their comrades about the idiocy of the odd couple shrinks!

I: Well, this has been most informative. You are both most unusual scholars and you certainly deserve your fame —and each other! Let me ask you both one final question: *What is going to be with you?*

They went for the groin!

## Chapter V  AGGRESSION CAN BE FUN

Just looking at you, I can see your problem. You're a "nice person" and if everyone doesn't dig you and dote on you, you get a little dotty. Under the "nice guy" patina (nice at home, nice at the office, nice at the club), you're seething with an unexpressed rage which has mucked up your whole personality. You smile and ingratiate and go along with real panache but the dirty little secret about you is that your anger is a small time bomb clicking away inside your head, waiting to explode. If you don't learn to face your very human aggressiveness—and to express it healthily —they're going to have to pick you off the wall some day . . . in pieces!

But, wait, help is coming.

*Creative Aggression* (by Bach and Goldberg) is a book that explodes our very American habit of judging a person by how much he (or she) smiles and how pleasant and "nice" the things he (or she) says. In our culture, the warmest praise one can inspire is that one is a "nice guy" or a "good guy." The "nice guy" is as American as apple pie, baseball, the Saturday night handgun, and the fast buck.

The authors demonstrate the great emotional damage we do to ourselves in repressing our natural anger and aggression. Relying on a host of case histories, they prove that a volcano of hostility seethes beneath the surface of "nice" parents, children, teachers, bosses, and even shrinks. This suppression of our natural rages is "crazy-making" and the proper solution is to use our aggression creatively and constructively, thus ridding ourselves of the mealymouthed artificiality of our relationships, opening us up to genuine intimacy. Notice how many killers are described by their shocked neighbors in the afternoon papers as "nice, pleasant kids." Unless we get with it, our buried aggressions can slowly drive us bananas. Fortunately for us, the authors aren't just spinning wheels. They have specific antidotes for us, like the following.

The author's theory of "constructive aggression on which ritual expression is based" is reduced to a simple formula:

$$AG(c) = \frac{II}{HH}$$

AG(c) = Constructive Aggression
II      = Informative Impact
HH    = Hurtful Hostility

The idea here is that constructive aggression improves as hurtful hostility is reduced. The authors dish out a series of devices aimed at increasing "informative impact" and triggering the safe discharge of irrational latent anger that leads to "destructive aggressive interaction." Here are a few:

### Vesuvius

Everybody in the group—staff, family, office, or whatever— agrees to let one member each time blow off steam, venting frustrations and irritations about the other members with no verbal response from the rest of the group. This is called "rage time," a few minutes of unrequited fury.

An inexperienced reader tried the "Vesuvius" in his department of Health, Education and Welfare, and it touched off the only government-sponsored mass pogrom in American history. No system is perfect. I, therefore, heartily commend "Vesuvius," but warn that there is also a "Samson Syndrome" in which the rager gets his destructive emotions out peachy cream but also tears down the entire institution in the process. Risk is part of life, that's all.

### The "Virginia Woolf"

This is a "free-for-all, no-verbal-holds-barred, below the beltline insult exchange between two people." It is conducted by mutual agreement for a definite predetermined time in order to clear the air of mutual resentments. This kind of slam-banging can be healthier than the delicate "walking on eggs" relationship because it involves deep commitment and security. There must be no physical violence in playing "Woolf."

No doubt the "Woolf" usually works out fine, but in our own experiments with Swedish WASPs in northern Minnesota we found it took us two years to thaw them out sufficiently to play. However, once God's frozen people got into it, they were usually excellent slam-bangers. However, there were some exceptions. One couple forgot to set a time deadline and mutually expired, after four years, of total exhaustion.

An interracial couple from Arizona, screaming vile epithets at each other, stimulated a race riot that stretched all the way to Cairo, Illinois. A Jewish couple in New York City got so militant that the Jewish Defense League built a whole chapter around them. Still another couple, both of whom were unalterably Listeners (see Chapter II), couldn't say any ugly or contemptuous things about each other, thus bringing them to the realization that they were not comfortable enough to rage at each other, so how could they truly love each other? They split, silently and sadly, as the hot molten lava of their Vesuvius just lay there, twitching slightly in the wind.

### Haircut with "Doghouse Release"

Adapted from a Synanon technique, this is a one-way scolding of an "offender" for any irritating behavior that is causing damage to the other person in the relationship. It's really a structured, quick catharsis. The "doghouse release" is a reentry ritual that can bring the offender back into the good graces of the other person. You can only give a haircut with permission of the other party—and with a time limit. You tell the "offender" you want to give him or her a "haircut" and, if he/she agrees, you lay it on him/her as he/she listens in silence to your complaint for a specific period of time (say two minutes). He/she cannot respond or defend him/herself nor engage in violence. If the "offender" assumes responsibility for an offense, you can give him/her a "doghouse release" and you must forgive and forget. If not, the "haircut" is kaput.

I tried the "haircut" on a cop who accused me (falsely) of jumping a red light. He seemed fascinated by the entire ritual, but he did not give me a "doghouse release" and neither did Bellevue Hospital to which he shlepped me, after laying on me a twenty-five-buck ticket for my "offense" (jumping the light). One must be careful in using the "haircut." Don't give one to strangers, muggers, or cops. One reader went to his best friend, who was bald as an egg (bald is beautiful), and asked to give him a "haircut" and, before he could explain the prohibition on violence, was hoisted and shackled on his own petard. Still another couple had such great success playing "haircut," which kept their marriage hairy and vigorous, that they installed a barber pole on their front porch, had sex on a barber chair, put a doghouse in their yard, and ate Alpo for lunch.

### Bataca Fight

This is my favorite Bach-Goldberg game. The bataca bats are cloth-covered and stuffed with a soft material. Thus the parties can swing at each other with all their power, like a pillow fight. Here, too, you must have mutual consent, a time limit (five years is too long) and you may have to give an "arms limitation" to the stronger party (like your grown son). Also, no hitting in the face or genital area, unless this is all-out nuclear war by prior agreement. Bataca fighting, the authors tell us, is a "safe, physical outlet for anger release, particularly when words fail them and tension exists (sic)."

Most marriages can truly be helped by bataca fighting. It is a big improvement over throwing flowerpots and Wilkinson swords. Drs. Surch and Distroy conducted experiments on bataca fighting in San Antonio. They found that the cultural and social environment had much to do with the tensions between individuals. For example, the community was up in arms about the attempt of an Arab sheik from Saudi Arabia to buy the Alamo as a birthday gift for one of his little princes named Onan. Bataca bats were booming in town during this controversy. Neiman and Marcus opened a San Antonio branch, featuring nothing but bataca bats. Enough steam was blown off to solve the energy crisis. The researchers found that "in most cases, the bataca fighting was salutary, emotionally satisfying and tension-reducing." But, alas, here too there were aberrations which may have something to do with the particular quirkiness of Texas. For example, one wife stuffed her bat with a live porcupine, perforating her husband's behind while getting her jollies. A husband negotiated an "arms limitation" with his wife which required her to fight on her knees while keeping her head in the oven. A son fought with his father on a high-wire over the Grand Canyon, eliminating once and for all the free-floating tension between them. Two madames of competing bordellos had a grand melee while their girls sold tickets for a good view from the upstairs windows.

Another researcher went to the Middle East, so persuaded of the efficacy of bataca fighting as a release from tension that he sought to induce the Arabs and the Jews to work off their anxieties in a massive bataca war. He was evacuated from a nest of guerrillas by Abie Nathan, who asked him to please keep his bats in the belfry.

When it comes to choosing between bataca fighting and "haircut," remember it is not either/or but both/and!

The authors clearly are on to something. Most situations we participate in are unreal rituals where we play our preordained parts, regardless of what we are really feeling. Take, for example, the latest "retirement party" at your office. It sounded like this as the president paid tribute to outgoing Sam:

### Farewell and Good Riddance

PRES: "Well, my cherished co-workers, I stand here with deeply mixed feelings today. On the one hand, we know that, after twenty-five years of distinguished service, Sam has richly earned the chance to retire and to spend time with his dear wife, Sally, and the cherished family he has, like all of us, neglected in the press of a distinguished career with the company. On the other hand, we will miss him dearly. He is as nice a guy as ever beat the drums in our p.r. department. He has given us the best years of his life and has performed with high capability, effectiveness, and good cheer at all times. So what can I say except God bless you, Sam, and you know that our hearts and doors will always be open to you. We wish you good health and much fulfillment. As a token of our great esteem, I want to give you this watch . . ."

SAM: "Thank you very much, Mr. Weathervane. My heart is too full to make a speech. But I want you to know that I leave here with a sense of great gratitude to you and all of my associates here at the company. This has been my life and I've enjoyed every minute of it. I now look forward, as Mr. Weathervane told you, to getting to know my family again, reading the books I've never had a chance to read, a little fishing, maybe a little writing that is a bit more challenging than a company press release—ha, ha—and reading the daily paper without worrying as to whether my release got printed or not. You are the finest bunch I ever worked with. I'll miss you. God bless you and thanks so much for your generous gift."

That's the script, the ritual, the role-playing. But, as the authors remind us, it's hokum. Those are not the *real* feelings. Let's try the same scene with the actors saying what is really churning in their minds:

PRES: I didn't think we'd ever get to this happy day. It took me a year to force Sam into early retirement. The nebbish had almost killed the department. He never could write a whole sentence in English, and he turned off every newspaperman in town with his anal iron-ass personality. Tim, his assistant, hated Sam's guts; he told me I had to choose between them, the company wasn't big enough for both of them. I couldn't stand having this character around all these years—he has the personality of a wooden Indian. I should have dumped him twenty years ago, but I wanted to be a "nice guy." If I had lowered the boom earlier, Sam would have had the sympathy vote of all the bleeding hearts in this loony bin. On top of all that, his wife, Sally, is a witch on wheels and she used to come to see me and threaten to blow the whistle on some of our company dirty tricks if we zapped Sam, whom she herself called a clown. I should have thrown her out on her ear, but . . . They deserve each other. I hope to hell they move west and get Californicated. He told his secretary that they expected airline tickets to Europe as the company gift. Maybe one-way tickets, if it had been necessary! If he doesn't like the watch, he knows where he can put it, or he can hock it if he needs to. Sam, just go already!

SAM: The only thing I want out of this company now is ME! I should have left here years ago, while I still had balls! After twenty-five years, I still have to call this phony MISTER Weathervane, even while he sticks it to me in front of God and everybody. The bastard never once called me into his office except to chew me out or to con me into resigning. Twenty-five years of making this crappy company look good, turning a sow's ear into a silk purse in a thousand stories they would have had to pay one million bucks to buy from an advertising agency. And for what? Who appreciates? That snake, Tim, has been greasing the skids for me for years, and he can't write one sentence in English. And now I have to stand up here and kiss their bottoms. For what? They think a cheap watch pays for twenty-five years of breaking my butt for them?

Bad as it was, I'm scared to death to leave. What will I do? How will I live? How much TV can I watch? Maybe I'll really write that novel about the "dirty tricks" of the company and all the heing and sheing that goes on in the executive suite. That would fix their wagons. Oh, boy, I'd love to see Weathervane's face when that came out. But, of course, I'll never do it.

So what do I look forward to now? Life with Sally? She'll badger me to death in two years. I didn't "neglect" her all these years; I *escaped* from her and thus saved our marriage, which could never have survived a real relationship. She thinks I don't know that she was seeing Weathervane on the side. Well, they *deserve* each other! Farewell, company, you took the best years of my life, and I was a horse's ass for giving it to you. And now, all my smiling and back-slapping associates, most of you are as phony as two-dollar bills and if I never see you again, it will be too soon! So kiss off!

Old Sam may have lost his job but at least he also lost his aggressions, and he did it without a bataca bat.

*Chapter VI*   **DON'T SIT IN WET
GRASS (TM)**

What you are suffering from is *ennui* stemming from an overdose of the frantic rat-race of modern life. Too much running, too much mouth traffic, too much fretting, too much wheel-spinning, too much thinking, too much aspiring. No wonder your head aches and you need a martini to quiet your gut at the end of the day.

Maybe you're in touch with the world, but you're obviously not in touch with yourself—the deepest, unfathomed depths of your being, your inner spirit. What you need to learn is how to empty your head of the cluttered accumulated debris of the day, to let your body float free and to refresh your soul with a draft of cool quiet. Frankly, the way things are going, you are a prime candidate for an ulcer, a coronary, or colitis or all of the above, unless you humanize yourself.

Try TM.

Some four hundred thousand Americans, as well as people from sixty other countries, have found self-help inside themselves through TM (Transcendental Meditation). TM is not a religion, though many of its devotees become chasidic in their dedicated zeal. It is actually a procedure for

getting tuned in to the deepest levels of your own personality. The technique was devised by Maharishi Mahesh
Yogi, founder of the TM movement. It derives from elements of the ancient Vedic tradition of India. Maharishi
immersed himself in Vedic study during a thirteen-year
vigil in the Himalayan Mountains. During this sojourn, he
became a disciple of the sage Swami Brahmananda Sara-
swati, Shancaracharya of Jyotir Math. Maharishi's army of
devotees refer to the Swami as the "grandfather" and master
teacher of the movement, Guru Dev.

The beauty of TM is that some scientists have placed
their kosher stamp of approval on it. Yale University maintains a Students International Meditation Society and some
scientists have studied the altered states of being fashioned
by TM and conclude that meditation is not only pleasant
but relieves tensions, heightens relaxation, and engenders
greater energy and alertness. For some people, it generates
exaltation and reduces anxiety.

Dr. Herbert Benson, a distinguished cardiologist at Har-
vard, has conducted a host of experiments as to whether
human beings were able to lower their blood pressure by
"thinking relaxed thoughts." While it worked better with
monkeys, real people did demonstrate physiological responses to meditation—responses which were greater than
those which might result from just sitting quietly with eyes
closed. Turned out that metabolism did slow down as much
as one might get from eight hours of deep sleep. The decline
in oxygen consumption was dramatic. People even sweated
less after meditation. Brain wave patterns differed. "The
whole picture that emerged," Benson told an interviewer

from the New York *Times* (Magazine Section, February 9, 1975, Maggie Scarf) "was that of a general quieting or damping down of the sympathetic nervous system." However, it turned out that TM could not reduce blood pressure enough to be curative or medically significant. Tough. So don't toss out your medication.

## Get Started

How do you get into TM? Find a TM group. There are three hundred and fifty TM centers throughout the United States. You'll be initiated in a thanksgiving ceremony performed in Sanskrit in front of an altar. Your initiator will stand alongside of you while you hold a flower. Your initiator will then give you your own lifetime secret mantra which, he insists, was especially chosen to match your particular nervous system, although cynics believe that it is picked haphazardly. Your initiator will then instruct you in the rules of TM, including:

1. Sit in a peaceful environment and in a quiet, comfortable position.

2. Relax all your muscles, starting with your feet and rippling through your body to the top of your head.

3. Breathe deeply through your nose. As you breathe out, recite your mantra, "thinking your mantra."

4. Continue this process for ten to twenty minutes. Do not use an alarm to terminate the meditation. When done, sit quietly for several minutes, first with eyes closed, then open.

5. Do your meditations twice daily and not within two

hours after any meal, because digestion louses up full self-relaxation.

TM really worked for me. But I had some problems. I despised my mantra—it reminded me of the sound my younger brother used to make when he had the dry heaves. Week after week I tried to get my initiator to change my mantra or my brother. No soap. Finally, I advertised in the *Village Voice* for an even trade with another TM dingaling, sight unseen, but there were no takers. Sadly, I resigned myself to my own awful mantra. And, miracle of miracles, it began to work and—now—I wouldn't surrender my mantra for all the tea in mainland China. And I wouldn't reveal it to any living soul, not even my brother-in-law who says that if I devoted the hours I now give to TM to writing, I would have already produced the Great American Novel. What does he know from fancy?

Mantras are supposed to be ancient, usually consisting of two syllables and sound like nonsense syllables. A good friend of mine has gone into the mass production of mantras and found that the following were his hottest commodities.

*Fancy Mantras*

YECH-YU          SHLA-MOZEL
SHENK-YU         GA-NIF
FIR-DRAY         TO-KAS
DRAY-KOP         VAZE-MIR
FIR-BLONDGET     OOI-GEVALT
SHMEN-DRICK      HOCKA-CHINA
GAY-COCKEN       KINA-HORA
OIS-KAMUTCHET

### My Own TM

When I first decided to put myself under TM, I sat out on the grass in the solitude of a green meadow on a soft spring day. I ran through the appropriate procedure and, in a matter of minutes, I sank into deep, soulful meditation. My mind seemed to float free. For some strange reason, however, I did not float *thought-free*. Indeed, my thoughts seemed to billow like fluffy clouds across a windswept sky, as follows:

This grass is wet . . . you couldn't at least sit on a *newspaper?* How can I think my mantra when my tush is soaked? What *is* my mantra again . . . ? Good thing I wrote it on my shirt sleeve . . . here we go . . . dumb mantra . . . oh, well . . . float into rest, deep and quiet . . . no fretting . . . forget about what that fink Ferguson said about your suit . . . what does he mean "looks like a daguerreotype of the 1920s"? . . . what the hell is a daguerreotype anyway? . . . that jlob doesn't exactly look dressed to the nines himself . . . keep your eyes closed . . . listen to the birds . . . really *listen* . . . hear the chirping—Watch out for *that bird!* . . . hear the cows in the distance . . . quiet down your body . . . hush up, feet . . . cool it, ankles . . . shh, thighs . . . settle down, pelvis . . . shush, hemorrhoids . . . tune down, shoulder blades . . . relax, jawbone . . . simmer down, eye muscles, avoid eye contact . . . lie flat, hairs—both of you . . . everybody tune down, down, down . . . like settling into a giant pillow . . . or disappearing into a deep, inky gorge . . . or drowning in a sun-splashed sea . . . drowning . . . *dying*.

Who would *cry?* . . . who would *care?* . . . serve 'em
right . . . they never appreciated me, really . . . let them
see I finally achieved something serious and definitive . . .
who will come to the funeral? . . . well, there are several
people I simply will not *have* at my funeral, that's final . . .
take Mike Demoto . . . when he sees me in the elevator, he
never says hello . . . looks right past me like I'm ectoplasm
. . . all he wants is to climb up in the pecking order, which
he should do very easily because he's the biggest pecker in
the plant . . . or Harriet Begin, the boss's secretary . . .
once she took my dictation and told everyone I was the
worst dictator in the building . . . oh, let 'er come . . .
dress up the place . . . but I definitely draw the line at the
big enchilada . . . he comes to my funeral only over my
dead body . . . in seventeen years at that place I never had
a single good word from him . . . every time I saw the boss
he gave me an earful of complaints. "What's wrong with
this, why so slow in that, why can't I do better with so and
so, blah, blah, blah" . . . keep him away or I'll jump out of
the box and belt him one in the head. He should only be
caught in the rain and turn to mildew . . . Now for my eu-
logy. Who could I trust with such a delicate chore? Probably
only Ralph. He's articulate, he has a mouth, but he'll end
up talking about himself, not me (an I for an I, a tooth for
a tooth). So I'll have to write it out for him.

Nothing pretentious—after all, I am a modest man and I
have much to be modest about. Nothing lugubrious—Helen
will be sad enough without Ralph coming on with sackcloth
and ashes. No, something graceful, slim and ripe, like that
new girl in the p.r. department . . . I think I'm getting
horny . . . what kind of meditation is this, for crying out

loud? . . . My thoughts are tumbling . . . bet my damn blood pressure is going up . . . I'm probably burning up oxygen . . . wish I could light up a cigarette but not with all this oxygen around. Stop it! Stop it! You're supposed to be zonked out on TM instead of getting soggy hemorrhoids in the grass and soft in the head!! Maybe it's something I ate—shouldn't have gulped down that pickled herring an hour ago . . . my initiator would really be pissed . . . is he really queer or is he *supposed* to hold my hand whenever he tells me about Vedic teachings? He can certainly come to the funeral—it'll show him what a truly *deep* meditation I finally achieved.

Meditation is associated with the Far East, but it is not the only—or maybe even the most potent—spiritual invention of the Asians. We learn from the New York *Times* of February 24, 1975, that the ineffable former President Nguyen Van Thieu of the former Republic of South Vietnam had mobilized the spiritual quality of "phuc duc" (sic), which, according to Stephen B. Young, former employee of the Agency for International Development, "demands that each individual Vietnamese be given an opportunity to lead a virtuous life, to receive the personal prosperity that comes as a reward for virtue, and to achieve a status commensurate with his innate, heaven-bestowed abilities." For years, we Americans tried to find out what we were fighting for, all up to our pupicks in the swamps of Vietnam. Now we know. It was to liberate phuc duc and to share it with the whole world. Wanna buy a phuc duc?

TM is good for people under fifty—over fifty, *BM* is better—but I think it's not as salutary as TLC (tender, loving care). TM is a solo job; TLC needs at least one partner.

Some say it is better to give TLC than to receive it, but that's bunk. You have to give it in order to receive it. TLC includes giving someone breakfast in bed, stroking your partner's ego, building someone up, and listening instead of talking. Shrinking your head sometimes works; TM often works. TLC *always* works, and while you don't have to get so close to your mate that you seem to be joined at the hip, you can't grow in a solitary vacuum, either. Together, nourishing each other with TLC, you can navigate the stormy shoals and get past the BS factor, with or without TM.

Besides, it may not be good for you to empty your mind through TM—how do we know it would ever fill up again???

## Chapter VII    WINNERS, LOSERS, AND NOCHSHLEPPERS

Have you ever wondered why your self-image is so *weak?* If others had the same image of you as you have of yourself, you would have the social life of a leper. Why do you *down* yourself so? What you need is to jazz up your lagging self-image. Why not *up* yours? Frankly, you've been a *loser* all your life precisely because you have *resigned* yourself to losing. You are a walking self-fulfilling prophecy. Where is it written that you must shlep through the rest of your life as woebegone and self-defeated as you've been up to now? Why do you nod so much your head falls off?

No, you've got to latch on to *personal growth*. You've rusted on your laurels long enough and the time has come for you to shift gears and take off, as a winner.

Personal growth is one of America's biggest growth industries. It is the *in* thing on college campuses, along with the growing popularity of majors in death and suicide. Maybe the world can no longer support the growth of production or of population, but there's plenty of room for us Americans to actualize our own potential. In a hefty, practical book entitled *Winners and Losers,* by Newburger and Lee, the key to such growth is placed in the lock and all you have to do is turn it. You do this by using PRS (Positive Reinforcing Statements) instead of NRS (Negative Reinforcing Statements). The following are examples drawn from the book:

PRS: Hey, I really put in a full day's work today.

NRS: There are four letters left. I'm always running behind!

PRS: Jim and the kids really loved the pie I made.

NRS: I'm sorry the crust wasn't more flaky.

If one constantly stresses the flakiness of his crust, one's ego finally becomes pasty. Thus one begins to become a loser. Unless one can train himself to SIM (Self-Image Modification), he will fall into a losing streak. A loser is someone who chronically fails to live up to his expectations of self. A winner is one who wins within his or her own framework of desires and capabilities. As the late Vince Lombardi used to point out, winning is not only better than losing, it is all there is! And losing, like smoking, is a bad habit. You can break it by modifying your own self-image.

The authors not only show you how to measure your self-image; they show you how to refurbish it. Nor is it the proverbial quick fix. No, they provide a comprehensive follow-through in which the reader takes an inventory test five times over a period of twenty-two months. All you have to do is keep a notebook during this period of gestation and put down the answers to three hundred questions. By checking the progress in successive tests, you can draw a learning curve of personal growth, thus maintaining a running inventory on how you are negotiating with your spouse, boss, children, and your cretin relatives.

Here are some examples of the author's true-false test, with my own responses and "modification-wise" comments:

|  | True/False | Modif-Wise |
|---|---|---|
| When I give advice, I want it followed. | T | Except by me. |
| People who are racially or religiously different from me can't become close because they don't speak the same language. | F | I hate them all regardless of race, color, or creed. |
| I think rich people are materialistic and probably crooked. | T | Poor people too. |
| Displays of anger ruin relationships. | T | That's why I get so violent against people who can't control their anger. |
| Drinkers are more fun than nondrinkers. | T | Better 1 W. C. Fields than 100 Richard Nixons. |
| The more people in my life, the better. | F | Ever been to Penn Station? |

| | | |
|---|---|---|
| I like cocktail parties because you can relate superficially. | F | No, because you can drink someone else's liquor. |

Unfortunately, the authors do not say which are the *correct* answers. However, if your answers correspond to mine, you are in trouble because I have rooted for the New York Mets since Marv Throneberry and Choo Choo Coleman, and I am not only a born loser, but enjoy it!

Friends have testified, from personal experience, that this system is marvy. It works. You can't prove it by me, however, I tried conscientiously—but always lost the damn notebook—once on an Eastern shuttle, once in the men's room of the Carousel Inn in Cincinnati, once during a pogrom at Shea Stadium, and once at the hands of a mugger in Chicago. However, I retained the notebook long enough to come to this conclusion:

Personal growth is good in moderation but, taken in too-large doses, you will find out who you *are* and maybe straighten your head a bit, but your job, your marriage, and your relationship to your children will go right down the tubes. The road to personal growth is littered with the shells of marriages and jobs which, while somewhat creaky and dubious to begin with, become intolerable when the feverish search for personal growth escalates. You may have a desire to uncover your inner voice, but if the only note that emerges is "mi-mi-mi," all the other singers will flee the stage sooner or later, leaving you at the center, singing your new-found heart out, but alone as a skunk on the trail!

Personal growth, then, is like perfume. OK to sniff and

to use to spruce yourself up. But gulp it down at peril to your health. So, herewith, the Vorspan self-inventory, to be taken once and then thrown away:

| *VSI* | True | False |
|---|---|---|

1. I like airplane food.
2. I often quit smoking.
3. My conversation is banal.
4. When I feel depressed, I could hit a cheery colleague in the snout.
5. I believe in capital punishment for double parkers.
6. I hate people who end every sentence with "don't you see . . . ?"
7. Nobody has let me complete a sentence in fifteen years.
8. Which is just as well, because I have nothing to say.
9. When I walk my dog, instead of thinking positively about what I'm doing for her

VSI                                    True        False

(PSI), I think guiltily
(NSI) about what
I'm doing to my
neighbor's lawn.

10. When I go to see a
football game and the
team huddles, I think
they must be talking
about me.

11. I put my wife on an
unlimited expense ac-
count, but she ex-
ceeded it!

12. I'm opposed to CIA
assassinations, but as
long as they are about
it, I have a little list.

The answer in every case is True and you get 8.5 for every
correct answer. If you got a score of 70 or below, you are
tearing yourself down too much. You certainly must build
yourself up because if you don't, who will? The key to a
good career, for example, is not *merit* or *brains*. It is *chutzpah.* If *you* believe you can do it and your image *conveys*
that confidence, the boss will *think* you can do it, and—ultimately—your associates will actually believe you're *doing*
it.

A friend of mine who cannot swim lucked into a job as a
swimming instructor, and was able to explain that he never
went into the water because he had seen *Jaws.* No matter

what the job you're applying for requires—language skill, steno, an eternal Ph.D., love of animals, experience with the Foreign Service—say *yes*. At the best, you'll learn quickly enough to survive. You may last twenty years, invisible in the interstices of the bureaucracy, turning your back each week while drawing your check. At worst, you'll be let go. So what? It's another entry to add to your variegated employment dossier.

Certainly do not be intimidated by lack of a college education. Education and college have only the remotest connection. Colleges have long since lost sight of their goals, and most of them are now inchoate factories, presided over absently by academic types obsessed with tenure, publishing or perishing, and ripe consultation plums. College graduates are prepared for nothing, except possibly graduate studies leading to a terminal Ph.D. Moreover, the student revolt of the sixties, which at least injected some drama into the college scene, has now wound down into malaise and torpor, occasionally enlivened by the spasm of excitement of an appearance by Lieutenant Calley, John Dean, or Ron Ziegler at the podium. College is supposed to be the molding of great minds and many are now very moldy indeed.

Your job is also not the place to look for personal growth. Jobs are basically nothing more than places to earn some bread and to protect us from our own sense of solitude. Many of us hurl ourselves into our work, becoming work addicts or workaholics in the process, burying our real selves in our careers. Yet, for most of us, our jobs are far from soul-satisfying, lacking inspiration, social fulfillment, and personal growth.

## Carry On, Porter

Taking inventory of ourselves may be, at worst, a harmless diversion. But, increasingly, Big Brother also seems to want to look inside our heads to see if we are losers or winners by *their* strange lights. Sylvia Porter, the economist, has reported that persons applying for various categories of federal employment have to take a test, including the following true-false questions:

|  | True | False |
|---|---|---|
| I go to church almost every week. | | |
| My sex life is satisfactory. | | |
| At times I feel like swearing. | | |
| I have used alcohol excessively. | | |
| I am very troubled by constipation. | | |
| I like poetry. | | |
| My mother was a good woman. | | |
| I do not always tell the truth. | | |
| At periods, my mind seems to work more slowly than others. | | |

What are we to make of such bureaucratic voyeurism? Picture the apparatchik in Washington who reads the application answers from a nice young woman from Ligen

Drerd, Indiana. "Mm, very interesting, but how can we match her self-image with the right job? Which job is best for a constipated woman who likes poetry and does not always tell the truth? Would you believe President of the United States? Or head of the FBI or CIA? Mmm, here's a racy one. Hey, Sam, what spot have we got for someone who likes airplane food, hates cold baths, and worries about premature ejaculation? Mmm, catch this one! Hey, Sam, here's a live one—a man who picks his toes, fantasies about circus clowns, and has a fear of nuclear bombs. Any opening for Senator?"

It is true that people tend to respond to us in accordance with our own self-evaluation. If you are a nochshlepper, pardon-me-for-living type and your boss calls you in to say you are getting no raise this year, you say thank you, I understand, because deep down you don't really think you are worthy and you're rather relieved he wasn't canning you altogether. The boss just took you at face value and, with a face like yours, it's no surprise you give yourself such little value. But if, on the contrary, you had a bit of self-esteem, it would rub off on all around you. It's not really who you know; it's who you *think you are.* I think I'm Attila the Hun, and the result is, nobody hassles me.

### Nipp and Tuck

The question arises: What about the self-image of those who test *our* self-image? Exactly who do the shrinks and test-makers think *they* are? The research of Osaka Nipp and Jeremiah Tuck is instructive on this question. The Nipp and Tuck inquiry found that of 100 shrinks interviewed, 93 were emotional wrecks. Nonetheless, 66 thought they were God, 12 thought they were merely doing God's work, 21 thought God was dead but if She came back She would be Jungian. One actually was God. The reason this doesn't total 100 is that the self-image of one male lay analyst had been artificially affected on the day of the interview by an untoward incident in which he was found nude in the bedroom closet of one of his female patients by the unanalyzed husband who, acting out, demanded to know what he was doing there. To which the lay analyst matter-of-factly replied: "Everybody has to be *somewhere*." Impressed with this explanation, the husband released the analyst, only to be presented with a forty-dollar bill for the hour in question ("I'm working any time my meter is running"), as a result of which the husband took the analyst to the backyard and totaled him.

Despite occasional demurrers in this chapter, evidence abounds that SIM (Self-Image Modification) can and does move mountains when followed rigorously. A young man in Yennavelt, Kentucky, passed from loser to winner in just three months, changing from a little-respected horse's ass in town to well-known jockey in the Kentucky Derby. A middle-aged woman nymphomaniac, who had buried five worn-out husbands (three of them her own) and whose present husband was no longer insurable, became a successful madame in the plushest bordello in Alaska, flourishing under a marquee which proclaimed: "We may be *cold* but we ain't *frigid*." There are many other success stories of languid losers who, having digested this book, began to zip through their lives as if they were double-parked. And—as you should know by now—this is potentially the *dynamite* period in your life, so get swinging.

Nonetheless the true way to be a winner—contrary to Newburger and Lee—is to be a gracious loser. Be an Adlai Stevenson, not a Spiro Agnew. Graceful losing builds character and inner strength. It is more educational than ten colleges.

France found its soul after its defeats in Algeria and Vietnam. America learned more about itself from losing Vietnam than we would ever have gained from winning. Martin Luther King grew in stature from suffering and anguish and the challenge of endless defeats, not to mention endless bugging by J. Edgar Hoover. The lust for winning leads us, ultimately, to a confusion of means and ends, to moral nihilism—to Watergate and worse. Life is not a baseball game or a tennis match, and competition is not man's noblest estate, and God will not look us over for medals, plaques, championship rings, and trophies, but for scars and bruises honestly earned in the struggle to be human and to give dignity to life.

The cult of success is one of the stigmata of American culture. William James said that "the exclusive worship of the bitch-goddess Success is our national disease." Nietzsche once said: "Success has always been a great liar." In American political life, as Arthur Schlesinger, Jr. (New York *Times* Magazine, June 21, 1975) has pointed out, losers have often left us a greater legacy than have winners; "Losers, as well as winners, identify problems, fulfill needs, and interpret emotions . . . the political process cannot be properly read as the simple annals of victory, of winners over losers." He reminds us of the enduring contributions of such losers as Bryan, Willkie, Stevenson, Goldwater, and McGovern, not to mention the disasters left to us by many recent winners.

So where does this leave you, a chronic loser? The only thing you've been able to beat consistently is your own ego. But you've still got your health and your good humor, and you still look snazzy in a Turkish bath. Don't bother looking for quick-fix remedies in everything from Freud to fatuous. Just live it up and *enjoy!*

*Chapter VIII*  **SEX THERAPY FOR GOD'S FROZEN PEOPLE**

Isn't it time for you to become reconnected to your body? The American Puritan tradition, now in shambles, has nonetheless cost us the ability to groove on our own bodies. We are God's frozen people, turned off to the pleasurable feelings of most parts of our bodies, and our senses are more dead than alive. Do we *know* how to make it all *feel*? Do we know how to ask for pleasures we want? How does our mate know we like to have the bottom of our feet detumesced if we don't ask? How does our mate know we like to be touched with a sheer scarf on our left shoulder-bone if we don't say so? Why do we avoid eye contact with strangers on an elevator? (Answer: Ever since that gorgeous stranger on the elevator caught your eye and said: "Look, we have only twenty seconds.")

You could go to a Human Discovery laboratory seminar, along with twenty other people, and spend a weekend getting in touch yourself. Here you will learn to "discard your past and future for two fun-filled days allowing the present to be deliberately and pleasurably expanded." Here you will be shown ways of combining what you already know with brand-new "sensory awareness exercises." Here "alternate life styles of tumescing are learned which are extraordinary additions to techniques that may currently be practiced." The goal: "To create active and passive situations so that each wins while the attentions and energies of both are focused onto one body." The laboratory you have selected is modeled after Masters and Johnson, including a "body inventory set at a structured pace."

In the laboratory, you will do such exercises as sitting on a mat with your partner and being touched on the most godforsaken parts of your body—earlobe, nostril, toe, knuckle, elbow—for six minutes after which your partner says thank you and then you reverse roles, you become active and your partner offers up his/her earlobe, etc.

Ideally, you will come out of the weekend more sensual and more sensitive, a better mate and an athletic lover. You may also come out jealous as a wet hen because your partner seemed to give off such good vibes while being stroked by jolly Frankie, whom you regard as a retarded ape. Ideally, you and your mate should have a ball Sunday night, but there is also a chance that, having fallen in love every twenty minutes (change of partner) throughout the laboratory, you overheated your radiator while your mate has come up cross-eyed from having monitored you over a shoulder and out of the corner of the eye for eight hours of exercises.

But with the economy going down the tubes, why pour one hundred dollars a person into such a weekend? After all, for a few more bucks—if you had it—you can hie yourself to the shore to get the same exercises in the nude, at least getting a good suntan (it shouldn't be a total loss) even if you never get reconnected to your body.

Not everyone can get reconnected with his body in one weekend. If your motor is coughing or your starter is misfiring, you may have to take your body in for a complete tuning by a surrogate wife or surrogate husband.

### Surrogate Mate

Borsht Kasha made a two-year study of the results of such reconditioning, and found a high rate of success. One man from New York went to St. Louis to work with a surrogate wife because he could not make it unless the Met game was playing at the top of the volume on television in the background. He was turned on by the voice of Lindsay Nelson. Naturally enough, his wife was put out. It wasn't only the six months of celibacy between seasons. It wasn't only that her husband's attention seemed to be distracted and that at crucial moments he would breathe: "Oh, God, I wish we had Tug McGraw back," or "Come on, Kingman, you longa lokshen, belt one!" It was the painful memory of that twenty-six-inning game at Shea which left her black and blue virtually to the All-Star game. "Enough," she said one open date, "this isn't normal. Go to St. Louis and take a surrogate wife, I wouldn't mind, and break yourself of this Met fetish!"

He went and—lo and behold—against all odds, his surrogate wife turned out to be a fanatical St. Louis Cardinal fan and, incredibly as it may seem (actually, he planned it, the devil!), the New York Mets were in town for the weekend! His therapy cost $2,200, plus travel, and at the end he was back to Square One, arriving home during the third inning of the Tuesday night game against Chicago, snapping on the TV set and balling his wife before she could finish washing the kitchen floor, while Bud Harrelson hit into an inning-ending double play. "But you're no different," she cried. "What happened?"

"Well, we tried to beat the habit by going to the game, but the surrogate wife and I ended up being barred from Busch Stadium for life!"

### Playing Around

However, according to a recent study, many Americans are getting their sexual therapy direct, rather than through the middle man. *Playing Around*, by Linda Wolf, consists of interviews with a variety of American women, each of whom has been involved in one or more extramarital affairs. It is clear to Ms. Wolf that, with the slippage of the old standards and the rise of feminism, together with the mounting tension of modern life, "playing around" has become virtually a new form of therapy for many persons, regardless of sex, race, or previous condition of servitude. And now that Betty Ford has put a kosher label on premarital affairs, our society is going to hell in a bucket.

Deeply shocked by the moral degradation involved in the suggestion that infidelity has virtually become an alternative —and acceptable—way of life, the Rev. Howard Andiamo, prominent religious sociologist, conducted his own research, designed to demonstrate that hi-fidelity is STILL the American way of marriage. Andiamo believed very frankly that Ms. Wolf found exactly what she was looking for and that, if you looked for faithfulness rather than "playing around," you would find it in abundance. Rev. Andiamo spent a week in the field, having been distracted in a cornfield in Moorehead, Minnesota, by a farmer's daughter before he got as far as the Twin Cities. His conclusions are arresting: 1. There are MILLIONS of Americans who continue to believe in the Sixth Commandment. 2. There are *some* Americans who actually *observe* the Sixth Commandment, notably an elderly couple in Des Moines and a modern equivalent of Bonnie and Clyde, a bandit couple from Seattle who are now confined—separately—in solitary in the Walla Walla Prison. Also two former film stars, each married eight times previously, now practicing continence and ostracized and exiled by Hollywood for "oddball behavior detrimental to property values in Hollywood." 3. The faithful couples were no more miserable than the unfaithful ones, whose affairs seemed to be conducted in a rather grim and joyless freedom. 4. In our culture, the OBSERVERS of the Sixth Commandment seemed to feel guiltier than its violators, a conclusion which Rev. Andiamo revealed with red-faced shame. 5. "Playing around" is becoming as common among women as among men, thus demolishing the ogre of the double standard which has plagued relations between males and females in America. 6. Widespread "playing around" has stimulated the economy, particularly the hot-bed special in motels, the large reclining back seat in imported cars, and the penance-dispensing capacity of the neighborhood shrink.

### In Africa

But, remember, you get nothing for nothing. We still must pay our dues sooner or later. Just recently—in Dahomey,

Africa—the President found his wife "playing around" with his Interior Minister and he had his guards execute the traitor while he was leaping, stark naked, over the fence. The Prime Minister then summoned an emergency meeting of the cabinet and took to television to explain to the nation that everyone must understand the full implications of the "revolution" and desist from fence-straddling and bed-hopping, especially in the Prez's bed. By the next morning, half the population of Dahomey had crossed the border into South Africa, where the revolution had already been, fortunately, canceled in advance.

As for you, let us say it flat out. Playing around is no solution to what ails you. You're a played-out lover, a worse liar, and your mate would know about the affair before your LOVER would, and you and your mate have been eyeball to eyeball for years and your mate has just been waiting for you to blink in order to justify starting up a separate but equal affair. Home is where the heart is. Don't start up.

### And at Home

Actually, the true chalutz (pioneer) of human sexuality is still Sigmund Freud, not those johnny-come-latelies of our time. Freud cut through all the barnacles of human nature and proclaimed that sex is the root of human behavior and that thwarted sexual development is the central source of neuroses. No Freudian dogma evoked such an uproar throughout the world as Freud's heretical teaching of the primacy of sexuality. In the generations which followed Freud, his disciples qualified him, arguing that he had overstated the sexual case, that sexual disturbance was only one of many root causes of emotional disturbances and that Freud had unwittingly oversimplified the mystery of the human equation.

But old Sigmund was probably right in the first place. Who can forget the play *Krapp's Last Tape,* in which a colorful old man, at the end of his life, savors the memories of his sexual adventures while ignoring the memories of literary and other successes?

The woods are chock full of self-help sex manuals, including *The Joy of Sex* and *What You Always Wanted to Know About Sex But Were Afraid to Ask.* But our independent sexologist, Borsht Kasha, has come up with his own empirical evidence which flies in the face of the conventional wisdom about human sexuality.

He conducted very unusual tests to measure at what age sex ceases to be vital to human behavior. He tested 750 persons seventy and over and, to his consternation, found no significant drop-off of interest in sex. One ancient witch chased Kasha around the table without falling off her broom. An ancient man described his recent visit to a bordello. "How old are you, anyway?" the madame asked him. "I'm ninety-three he said. "Well, you've had it, sir," she told him. "I have? Oh, then how much do I owe you?"

Of the 750 old persons examined, 500 continued to enjoy sexual activity. Of those whose sex lives had come to an end, none attributed the decline to advancing years. Two hundred blamed gas or the stomach; twenty said they could not find a hotel on Medicare; fifteen said they would have an affair but they didn't want to have to write a "thank you" note afterward; five thought they would lose their welfare checks; one suffered from 150 per cent command impotence and now got his jollies from soft porn; and one had been dead for a week.

In the olden days, sex was regarded as marital procreation; today it is mostly regarded as recreation. In those days, sex was intended to perpetuate the family. Well, sex has flourished, but whatever happened to the *family?* Where did it go? Exactly what *is* it?

### Whither the Family

Once it was simple nuclear—mother and father and 2.6 children, with four grandparents. But now? What with divorce zooming off the scope and new patterns of mating without marriage, and marriage without children, the family is adrift. What happens to the family when the husband is now into his second wife who has already run through three husbands, with nine miscellaneous children scattered across the landscape as a result of these varied interpersonal transactions? Which of these kids are *mine?* Which are *yours?* Which are *ours?* Are the various husbands rivals or members of a broadening mishpocheh (family)? How does one designate his second wife's third husband? The Family needs a Vatican Council to pull itself together and redefine mothering, fathering, and family.

Problems abound. What about the new-breed "Breeder"? She is the sophisticated modern woman who chooses not to marry but, wishing to be a mother, selects a man with superior genes to mate with, producing maybe a biologically superb child, but the man disappears from view once his task is done, never to see its fruit. What is the *family?* Who is the *father?* Is the *mother* also the *father?* What, indeed, is going on here? Nobody knows nor does anybody know where it will all lead, and you can't tell the Family without a scorecard.

The family has been, historically, the font of values, the true shrine of human love. Today it is splintering like a damaged oak. We family folk who cherish the family unit can only hunker down and pray to God that She restores the Family in its pristine faith, for better or for worse.

We called on our favorite sexologist, Dr. Borsht Kasha, and we put the tough questions right on the line.

### A Scientific View

"Doctor," we said, "where will this sex revolution end? First, sex got split off from marriage, now it is split off from love. It seems to be becoming a social hour—mechanical thing—and now straight sex seems to be going out in favor of funky, bizarre sexual patterns.

"Everybody's playing around, it's terrible, like ancient Rome," murmured Dr. Borsht Kasha.

"Then you don't approve, Doctor? Well, I feel a little better. I thought it was just I who was behind the times."

"No, indeedy," said Dr. BK. "It's crazy, all this feely-touchy stuff, these nudes slopping in the mud, the groupie movement, the orgies, the homosexuals. It's decadent, that's what it is. The sexual revolution is killing sex. Robespierre is in the saddle!"

"I certainly agree with you, Dr. BK. But is there no way to restore the old traditional values of marriage, fidelity, love, moderation? I mean, must it be this way?"

"Listen," he replied, "my mother used to say: a pogrom

is a pogrom. When in Rome, do as the Romans do," and he departed to cruise a gay bar.

Actually, the *BS Factor* operates most powerfully in sex self-help courses. Many of the leaders—like our own Dr. BK —are screwed up sexually themselves; like the unconsciously prurient who makes a career out of fighting "dirty movies," many of the self-appointed sex experts are themselves funky about sex and emotionally twisted like a pretzel. You and your mate can help yourselves without going into hock or becoming mechanical acrobats by the numbers. Love, not technique, is the ticket. Tenderness, not scenarios, is the path to fulfillment. Marital sex is still the most potent invention since the wheel, and most of us are so busy fantasizing about Robert Redford and/or Raquel Welch that we abandon the richest natural resource for human development and emotional fulfillment. Charity begins at home, and so does true sexual adventure. It's old-fashioned and corny and sounds bland next to hot visions of a wild Technicolor orgy. But the secret of sex is not the explosive bliss of the one-night stand; it is the glow the morning after and the shaping of a deep, growing relationship. That's the real marriage encounter!

## Chapter IX

**MACROBIOTICS DIET
AND THE NOSHER'S DIET
OF DR. WATKINS I
PRESUME**

Your problem may, perchance, have nothing to do with your personal relations or how your head is working. It could be what you *eat*. Maybe, as it is sometimes said, we are what we *eat*. Dr. George Ohsawa, an Oriental philosopher-scientist, is the chief guru of macrobiotics, which consists primarily in the avoidance of extreme yin (vitamin C) in our daily diets. Ohsawa cites the good health of the Eskimos, who avoid foods that are rich in vitamin C, such as lemons, oranges, tomatoes, and pineapples. "In spite of this, not a single case of scurvy has ever been detected among them," he reports.

Ohsawa teaches that there are two fundamental ways to become healthy, free, and happy: (1) raising our judgment to the highest level through awareness of absolute truth; (2) dietary discipline which conforms to the law of change (the unifying principle of yin and yang). A strict diet of grains—or of grains and vegetables—can be healthful in finding awareness of absolute truth (oneness). But stay away from fruit. It's poison.

## Down with Fruit

Here are excerpts of comments by Neven Henaff, Ohsawa's first European disciple (Ignoramus Library Report, *Vitamin C*, by Neven Henaff, and *Fruit*, by George Ohsawa, Ohsawa Foundation, Inc.), about the danger of fruit and the folly of fruitarians:

"Give fruit to a child who is a habitual bedwetter and he will perform on schedule that very night . . .

"Ninety per cent of the individuals who suffer from excessive loss of hair are people who love fruit. Those who do not regularly eat fruit can try a pear or a peach to prove to themselves that ten times more hair than usual will be in their combs the very next morning.

"Those who eat fruit all the time have no sexual desire. Those who have a more or less yin constitution, either by birth or as the result of a fruit diet, forget about sex forever. They become more and more religious and consider sexuality hateful and loathsome . . .

"A fruitarian community or country is gradually depopulated. This is obvious if we study a population (demographic) map . . .

"In the United States where polio has been of epidemic proportions, the polio *virus* (?) has been exorcized with DDT strewn from planes . . . but actually the malady has been distributed in the streets by unknowing fruit vendors . . .

"Fruitarian monkeys and gorillas are, in reality, mongoloid homo sapiens . . .

"Those who love fruit, and continually eat much of it,

eventually become suspicious, jealous, fearful, indecisive; are easily chilled and prone to heart ailments . . .

"Fruitarian women suffer from deformities of the uterus and menstrual irregularities . . .

"Cancer victims are almost always those people who love sweets and eat fruit in quantity . . .

"I suggest that you verify my theory by experimenting on yourself or by giving someone one or two pieces (one-quarter to one-half pound) of fruit every day for a length of time. You will see an undeniable tendency toward cardiac hypertension in a short time.

"If there *is* some benefit, some profound and lasting good result, I will commit hara-kiri."

This may seem strange to modern, western man. But the author himself is proof of Henaff's theories. I have been a fruitarian since the age of three months. My parents told me that, as a baby, I subsisted on bananas. This banana fetish continues to this day; I can consume a dozen bananas during a Noxzema commercial and I eat bananas with strawberries, with peanut butter, fried, baked, boiled, frittered, or roasted. In addition, I have a voracious appetite for fruits of all kind. The result is—believe it or not—I lost my hair before I became a thirty-year-old fruitarian. If that isn't proof, what is?

Dr. Mack Learner's research demonstrates that putting a staple in your ear is equally effective.

Napoleon said an army fights on its stomach. It is said we are what we eat, whether we are soldiers or civilians. Baloney, I am a banana, you are a fruitcake, and my shrink is a cactus (tough on the outside, soft inside). And, in

America, our life-style is shaped by a reckless overeating which is bad for our figures as well as our health. Thus, dieting and weight-watching have become national obsessions. Until recently, dietary self-abuse was a personal matter. Today, however, in a world in which famine has become an international way of life, it is sinful for us to gorge ourselves while half the world is hungry. Millions of Americans are today following one or another popular regimen to trim down our surplus blubber. A good thing, too, because waste of food is no longer merely gross; it is antihuman.

Thus, we seize every diet nostrum that comes down the pike, whether it is water diets, vegetarianism, weight watchers, or Dr. Atkins' diet. Each has its following and its record of quickie successes, but we have one than which there is no whicher.

### Up the Nosher's Diet

It is the Nosher's Diet, as worked out laboriously in a Tel Aviv noshatorium by Dr. Watkins I Presume. It has the virtue of simplicity, proved effectiveness, and it permits you to eat three meals and seven noshes a day without becoming either a fat cow or a common crank. Here is the Dr. Watkins I Presume Noshing Diet for one day (putting a staple in your ear also wouldn't hurt):

You sleep until noon and have brunch in bed on the theory that everyone has to be somewhere.

Noon brunch: gator juice, chicken soup, 1 slice of unbuttered matzo, 3 raisins, 1 bowl of Alpo with fresh berries in season, 1 cup decaffeinated coffee.

2:00 P.M.: 1 banana, 1 dozen steamers, chicken soup.

3:00 P.M.: 1 falafel, pitta, chicken soup, and peasant under glass.

4:00 P.M.: chicken delight.

5:00 P.M.: send out for Chinese (spareribs, lobster cantonese, and fried rice). Choose 1 from column A and 2 from column B.

6:00 P.M.: Start with St. Jacques's roast stuffed camel* (roasted slowly over an open fire), chicken soup, UFW lettuce, sliced tomatoes, Carvel ice cream, tea (one teabag for 3 glasses; never drink tea out of a cup, it causes onanism), ding dong food, roughage.

7:30 P.M.: Howard Johnson's fried clams and a bottle of Heineken's beer, chicken soup.

9:00 P.M.: chicken soup, linguine and clam sauce (only white), a slice of halvah.

11:30 P.M.: something light, to sleep by, like chicken soup; a large salami sandwich on a hard roll, hold the mustard; borsht and kasha (don't mix them).

We have, of course, checked out the Dr. Watkins I Presume diet and our research indicates very gratifying results, quite comparable to most other well-known diets. Of some hundred subjects, twenty-three lost at least five pounds and two got pregnant—one woman and one man. Some twenty-nine gained weight, but they carried it well. Two got so fat that they had to be picked up by a crane. One Jewish woman got very sick on the Arab food—a bad

---

* In *The Great Escape: A Source Book of Delights and Pleasures for the Mind and Body,* Yee and Wright tell us this is served at Bedouin wedding feasts and requires 200 hard-boiled eggs, 100 gutted Mediterranean trout, 50 cooked chickens, 1 roasted sheet, and 1 camel.

case of Pharaoh's Revenge. One unfortunate subject choked on the Alpo, but his bark was worse than his bite. Seven persons got so hooked on this diet that they quit their jobs and "tripped" out. One woman, who has an IQ of 83 on a hot day, gained weight and quit and now her diet consists of eating her heart out with nostalgia. All in all, a qualified success, now pending before the FDA, and most of the subjects are now healthy as Hunzas!

It is clear, however, that what runs thickly through the Dr. Watkins I Presume diet is chicken soup. All else can be dispensed with—the chicken soup is the secret of élan vital and fine tuning of the system, as the following medical paper on "Chicken Soup Rebound and Relapse of Pneumonia: Report of a Case," by Nancy L. Caroline, M.D., and Harold Schwartz, M.D., proves conclusively.

### Right on with Chicken Soup

A case is reported in which a previously healthy individual, having received an inadequate course of chicken soup in treatment of mild pneumococcal pneumonia, experienced a severe relapse, refractory to all medical treatment and eventually requiring thoracotomy. The pharmacology of chicken soup is reviewed and the dangers of abrupt termination of therapy are stressed.

Chicken soup has long been recognized to possess unusual therapeutic potency against a wide variety of viral and bacterial agents. Indeed, as early as the twelfth century, the theologian, philosopher, and physician Moses Maimonides wrote, "Chicken soup . . . is recommended as an excellent food as well as medication." Previous anecdotal reports regarding the therapeutic efficacy of this agent, however, have failed to provide details regarding the appropriate length of therapy. What follows is a case report in which abrupt withdrawal of chicken soup led to severe relapse of pneumonia.

### Case Report

The patient is a forty-seven-year-old male physician who had been in excellent health until eight days prior to admission, when he experienced the sudden onset of rigors followed by fever to 105° F. He was seen by a physician at that time, when physical examination revealed a severely toxic man, unable to raise his head from the bed. Pertinent physical findings were limited to the chest, where rales were heard over the right middle lobe. Chicken soup was immediately begun in doses of 500 jlpoq 4 hours. Defervescence occurred in thirty-six hours and a chest x-ray film taken five days prior to admission was entirely normal. Because he felt symptomatically improved, the patient declined further chicken soup after this time. He continued to feel well and remained afebrile until the night prior to admission, when he developed right upper quadrant pain, nausea, and vomiting while on a visit to Vermont. His vomiting persisted through the night, and the following morning when he boarded a plane for Cleveland, he was cyanotic and in severe respiratory distress.

He was brought immediately to a hospital where physical examination revealed an acutely ill man, febrile to 104° F., breathing shallowly sixty times per minute, with a pulse of 140. Physical findings were again chiefly limited to the chest, where bilateral pleural friction rubs, bibasilar rales, and egophony over the right middle lobe were heard. Chest x-ray examination showed consolidation of the right middle lobe, infiltrates at both bases, and a questionable right pleural effusion. White cell count was 7700 without a shift to the left. Electrolytes were within normal limits. Arterial blood gases on 6 liters/min of nasal oxygen were PH=7.51, Pco2=20 torr and Po2=50 torr. Gram stain of the sputum showed swarming diplococci, and multiple cultures of sputum and blood subsequently grew out type 4 Pneumococcus. Chichen soup being unavailable, the patient was started on one million units q 6 hours of intravenous penicillin. Failure to respond led to increases of the dose up to 30 million units daily. Nonetheless, the patient remained febrile and his chest x-ray showed progressive effusion and infiltration. On the twelfth hospital day he was taken to the operating room for a right thoracotomy. He thereafter made an uneventful recovery, maintained on 30 million units of penicillin daily during his postoperative course, and was discharged on the twenty-fifth hospital day.

## Discussion

The therapeutic efficacy of chicken soup was first discovered several thousand years ago when an epidemic highly fatal to young Egyptian males seemed not to affect an ethnic minority residing in the same area. Contemporary epidemiologic inquiry revealed that the diet of the group not afflicted by the epidemic contained large amounts of a preparation made by boiling chicken with various vegetables and herbs. It is notable in this regard that the dietary injunctions given to Moses on Mount Sinai, while restricting consumption of no less than nineteen types of fowl, exempted chicken from prohibition. Some scholars believe that the recipe for chicken soup was transmitted to Moses on the same occasion, but was relegated to the oral tradition when the Scriptures were canonized. Chicken soup was widely used in Europe for many centuries, but disappeared from commercial production after the Inquisition. It remained as a popular therapy among certain Eastern European groups, however, and was introduced into the United States in the early part of this century. While chicken soup is now widely employed against a variety of organic and functional disorders, its manufacture remains largely in the hands of private individuals, and standardization has proved nearly impossible.

Preliminary investigation into the pharmacology of chicken soup (Bobbymycetin) has shown that it is readily absorbed after oral administration, achieving peak serum levels in two hours and persisting in detectable levels for up to twenty-four hours. Parental administration is not recommended. The metabolic fate of the agent is not well understood, although varying proportions are excreted by the kidneys, and dosage should be appropriately adjusted in patients with renal failure. Chicken soup is distributed widely throughout body tissues and breakdown products having antimicrobial efficacy cross the blood-brain barrier. Untoward side effects are minimal, consisting primarily of mild euphoria which rapidly remits on discontinuation of the agent.

While chicken soup has been employed for thousands of years in the treatment of viral and bacterial illnesses, there have been no systematic investigations into the optimal course of therapy. The present case illustrates a possible hazard of abrupt chicken soup withdrawal: a previously healthy man, having received what proved to be an inadequate course of chicken soup for clinical signs of pneumonia, experienced a virulent relapse into severe bacterial pneumonia. It was not possible in this case to determine whether the relapse was caused by resistant organisms, as chicken soup was unavailable at the time treatment had to be restarted, and a synthetic product of lesser potency was used instead. Further study is needed to determine the most efficacious regimen for chicken soup. Pending such investigation, it would probably be more prudent to give a ten-day course at full dosage, with gradual tapering thereafter and immediate resumption of therapy at the first sign of relapse.

Reprinted with permission of *Chest,* the Journal of Circulation, Respiration, and Related Systems. February 1975.

*Chapter X*  **ASSERT YOURSELF; IT'S LATER THAN YOU THINK**

Are you tired of being pushed around? Are you always the one to give *in*—never the one to stand *up* for yourself? Do you feel cowed by salesmen, conductors, policemen, secretaries? Is it impossible for you to *assert* yourself?

Why is it you never add up your bill in the restaurant? Why overtip? Why do you never open your mouth when the TV man charges you ten dollars for a house call which turned your *snowy* picture into a *blizzard?* Why do you never stand up to your Mandarin boss who treats you as if your office was a tiger cage, and then you blow off steam at home at your bewildered mate? Why do you let your child treat you as if you were Archie Bunker? Why do you let the salesman pick your clothes? Why don't you knock down the insolent uncle who gets his jollies making fun of your waistline and your waddle? Why do you tip when the service was abominable? Why don't you bang on the wall of your hotel room when your neighbor seems to be presiding over a combination of wild orgy and pogrom? Why do you just sit there with your ear pressed to the wall?

Nobody will protect your dignity if you allow yourself to be turned into the neighborhood Persian rug. Get with it.

You don't have to be obnoxious to tell the salesman to bug off, your boss to get off your back, your uncle to get lost, the TV man to expect a visit from Betty Furness and the Better Business Bureau, to have a long chat with your kid the day he expects his allowance (a little blackmail goes a long way).

Women's liberation has done wonders for the assertiveness of women. Millions, who once followed their husbands ten paces back like Mary's little lamb, have grown to respect themselves and to defend their personhood. Now, if the husband asks for his dinner, the little woman is likely to explain, "Up yours!" Nebbish men are being inspired to emulate their newly liberated women.

### An Apocryphal Tale

One of my friends refused to take yes for an answer in life, and decided he had to assert himself, too. He had a fine broth of a wife, three shiny-faced kids, a nice home, they both had good jobs and a pleasant life. But he insisted on "growing" as a person and asserting his personality. "If I don't make an effort constantly to grow, I'll shrivel up and die inside," he told her. Delighted with himself for drying the dishes and helping his wife set the table, he encouraged her to join a NOW Consciousness Raising group and she grew in self-understanding, so much so that she gave up her secretarial job ("I'm not going to be a go-fer and a coffee-maker for some male chauvinist all my life") and then couldn't find a job which conformed to her broadened self-image. He hied himself to a shrink and *grew* in insight, although the fat bills put the family into a financial wringer.

He then shlepped his wife to Marriage Encounter—"If we don't truly *grow* together, we'll surely grow apart"—and they achieved so acute a level of communication (which they had been spared throughout ten years of married life) that they separated and he moved into a Manhattan apartment, nicely furnished with the Marriage Encounter leader. Undaunted, he slogged on—"I have to find out who I am as a *man* and a *person;* I have to grow as a *human being,* then all else will fall into place"—and he developed such a rage at his boss and his colleagues ("They don't respect my unique personhood, my identity") that he suddenly found himself the subject of an office goodbye party (see Chapter V).

Refusing to stop *growing,* even in the face of his palpable successes, he "found God" at the kitchen table in the middle of a lonely scotch-filled night, and God's voice directed him to take his rusty hunting rifle and dispatch his ex-wife while *growing* in the saddle of the Marriage Encounter counselor. When I last heard from him, he was deeply "into" Weight Watchers at the state prison—and he had grown to a formidable 275 pounds.

Growing old is easier than growing up; and sometimes we should let sleeping dogs sleep.*

### Say No

There is a better way to learn to assert yourself, without going bananas. The book, *Don't Say Yes When You Want to Say No,* by Fensterheim and Baer, will help to put some steel in your spine.

---

* My own wife has dissociated herself from this chapter, which she regards as "pure chauvinist hokum." I have not let her read the rest of the manuscript.

The book's ads promise you will learn how to:

* Ask for your money back and get it.
* Say NO to a persuasive salesperson, uppity children, and a tight-assed boss.
* Demand your rights.
* Cope with "put-downs."
* Get rid of self-consciousness.
* Get promotions and raises.
* Stop with those hurt feelings all the time.
* Find spontaneity in sex.
* End a phone conversation when YOU want to.
* Be ASSERTIVE, not aggressive.
* Like yourself a lot better; and
* Improve memory, reduce weight, tension and other "killer habits."

I took the Assertiveness Training program myself and it worked wonders for me. Until I took it, I was the shlemiel type, pardon me for living, needing everybody—including waiters and conductors on the Long Island Railroad—to love me. I NEVER said NO. I was miserable. It always rained on my parade. But now, get this, I am a truly AS-SERTIVE sonofabitch and my problems are solved. Where I used to be MISERABLE, now I make everyone else MIS-ERABLE. I NEVER approve the wine which the waiter pours after I select my Poisse or Bova. Let him work for his tip, which I also have reduced drastically. I do not stand still for a putdown any longer. I smile and say: "Listen, all your teeth should fall out except *one*, and that *one* should give you a *toothache!*"

I stood up to a mugger in Central Park and spent seven assertive weeks in Lenox Hill Hospital. I NEVER kiss my boss's behind any longer, no yes man I; instead, I gleefully bring him espionage reports of how other employees poormouth him in the elevator. I am no longer merely acquiescent in my sex life. NOW I am so SPONTANEOUS that I often start without her. I no longer CARE what others think, and that works fine because since I got ASSERTIVE I am avoided like the plague anyway. I no longer nod so much my head falls off. And I NEVER get talked into doing things I don't want to do any more; no, I have announced to friend and foe alike that I don't want to do ANYTHING except stay home and work on my memory and try to recall what it was like to have friends, loving relatives, and a close family. I am now assertive and OK and a true pain in the neck!

### The Ultimate Test

How do *you* know when you are becoming adequately assertive? Easy. Go into an elegant restaurant in New York. When the headwaiter sniffs you, as if you were something the cat dragged in, and begins to lead you to the table next to the men's room, stuff a bill in his hot hand and say: "We'd like to sit at that nice table over in the corner with the 'Reserved' sign on it." Then, once seated, when two waiters hang on your shoulder waiting for your order, just lean back and say: "We'll be a while yet. Don't call me; I'll call you." Now ask him to ask the chef to make a fettuccine that is not on the menu and have the wine steward earn his keep looking for your '46 Bordeaux. When the Venetian fettuccine is served, taste it and proclaim, "Feh!" And when you finish your coffee, don't let the headwaiter pull your chair right out from under you when he drops the check in your dessert. Say: "We'll relax over cigars now, thank you." Then, in a leisurely mood, check the bill, placing your little calculator on the table and totting up the figures. "My good man," you say, snapping your fingers, "I believe there is a slight error." Don't let them intimidate you. Assert yourself. Don't ingratiate. Display some macho for once. After dinner you'll feel ten feet tall and your dinner companions will regard you as a nouveau sonofabitch!

People can be divided between those who can *never* assert themselves by taking the initiative to end a phone conversation and those who *are assertive every time*. I have a friend who is so congenitally unable to break off a conversation that she once, upon receiving an obscene telephone call, listened patiently to thirteen and a half hours of heavy breathing until the nut on the other end simply ran out of gas. Her husband, on the other hand, is like a traffic controller, terminating every conversation at the moment of his choice. When someone came to the door to try to get him to sign a petition denouncing the mayor for having three brothers-in-law on the public payroll, our hero cut him down with: "Look, nepotism is OK so long as it's kept in the family."

If you are the first type—who cannot break off a conversation—all you need to do is memorize the following battery of non-sequiturs and drop one in judiciously in the middle of a conversation—and depart.

1. Do you know your charisma is hanging out?
2. Our child psychologist is seven years old.
3. My doctor is half-boy, half-swine.
4. Stay as loose as a goose.

5. Have they given you a saliva test?

Don't be a doormat any more. Remember what Benjamin Franklin once said: "Behold the turtle. It makes progress only when it sticks out its neck!"

## Chapter XI

**GAMES PEOPLE PLAY
AND THE BS FACTOR**

"Don't play games with me." No doubt that put-down
has been put to you—and by you—on many exasperating oc-
casions. But it's bum advice. For the truth is that we all play
games with each other most of the time.

Some of us feign illness to get attention. Others use emotional blackmail to extort "love" and to get our way. Some
of us provoke our mates to start a fight so we can then feel
righteous in going off to bowl with the gang. Some of us
have a penchant for steering the conversation to precisely
those subjects on which we can grab center stage. Some of
us manipulate our children by judicious ladling of guilt ("I
see you are wearing one of the two ties we gave you. What's
the matter, you don't like the other one?"). Some of us
have an elaborate scenario of manipulation as a prelude to
—or substitute *for*—lovemaking. Some of us like to play
"Ain't It Awful" or "Everybody's Out to Screw Me" (the
fact that you're a paranoid doesn't mean they're *not* trying
to screw you!) or "One-Upmanship" or "King of the Hill."

Dr. Eric Berne, in his fabulously popular *Games People
Play,* has given us some provocative and revealing games.
But, you should forgive me, I have some I like better. One

is called "What Would You Do If?" and here are some examples:

### What Would You Do If

1. A person of the opposite sex rushes up to you as you are dining with your spouse at a restaurant. The person plants a big kiss on your mouth, embraces you warmly, and expresses delight at seeing you again after all these years. "You remember me, don't you?" You don't have the faintest recollection who it is. What do you do?

   a. Say, "You'll have to forgive me, but I don't remember who you are."

   b. Keep eating.

   c. Say, "If you don't, why should I?"

   d. Sweat.

   e. Realize that the intruder has bet a friend ten bucks that he/she could kiss a total stranger (and you have to admit you are stranger than most).

2. You come outside and find your car blocked by a double-parked car.

   a. You wait patiently.

   b. Double-park your own car and go into the saloon for a double martini.

   c. Honk your horn.

   d. Go into your TM number (See Chapter VI).

   e. Push his car over a cliff.

3. A young woman comes to your door and tells you she is raising funds for the wife of the unknown soldier. How do you react?

4. You are raped on the Long Island Railroad.

a. Compel your fellow passengers to put down their newspapers and realize what happened, those zombies!

b. Tell the conductor not to let anyone off the train.

c. Announce that the culprit will be charged not only with rape, but, inasmuch as it happened on a train, also with a moving violation which, unlike rape, goes on his driver's licence.

d. Change at Jamaica.

5. You are eating your lunch on the plane when the pilot announces that one engine is on fire.

a. Give back your lunch.

b. Pray.

c. Send an ESP message to your shrink, Dr. Rock Rega.

d. Tell your seat partner you are not afraid of flying, only of crashing.

6. You and your spouse are driving home from a party. The silence is oppressive. Suddenly your mate explodes: "Dammit, I've never been so humiliated. Do you know how you made me feel in front of all those people when you said . . . ?"

a. Plausible deniability.

b. Say, "Look, you're too thin-skinned."

c. Purse your lips and lie through your teeth.

d. Jump out of the car like Evel Knievel.

e. Use this as an opportunity to communicate without seeking to assess who was "right" and "wrong."

The right answer is e., but the most effective (although immature) is d., unless you are driving over a narrow bridge.

### Going to Meetings (GTM)

One of the crucial games we Americans play is GOING TO MEETINGS. Voluntarism is a hallmark of American life, and there are organizations of citizens to achieve everything from free vasectomies to noise abatement, to selling the Nixon tapes to Muzak. De Tocqueville, a century ago, noted the fever of citizen involvement in pioneer America; despite the lumps of cynicism we've all taken in recent decades, most Americans are still joiners and belongers. The organization, club, committee, workshop, and seminar are American devices for grass-roots democracy. They may also reflect our inchoate yearning for a sense of community, our answer to alienation, fragmentation, and TV. Whatever the *genesis,* there is an *exodus* to meetings in virtually every American home. Indeed, many of our high-priced executives spend most of their time at staff meetings. As a survivor of 12,741 meetings—at which 9,474 corned beef sandwiches were consumed and 12,699 notes were distributed by me alone—I am highly qualified to make the following observations about the Games We Play before, at, and after meetings.

Firstly, you must know that the real agenda takes place *before* the meeting. The purpose of the meeting is to put a formal seal on the wheeling and dealing which takes place in advance of the meeting. This is especially true of fund-raising meetings, where "new" money is generated in peer-to-peer contacts well in advance of the official occasion. A good professional or president never goes into a meeting unless he/she knows exactly what will come out of the meeting (besides himself). This is called GETTING YOUR DUCKS IN LINE and it has more to do with logrolling and back-scratching than the pure elemental processes of democracy, which is a nice notion but can kill a meeting with seven simultaneous motions and three contradictory amendments, plus a motion to table, irritating everyone and dooming any action right off the top. The inside group must do its "homework," count its noses in advance, mobilize its troops, exercise its muscle, and produce a quid for its quo, which is the name of the game.

Going to too many meetings is a form of cruel and unusual punishment, but veteran meeting-goers learn how to cushion the shock to the system without becoming over-workshopped. One popular way is not to listen and to sit quietly doing needlepoint. This course can be pursued, but only if you make sure to sign the attendance sheet and also to rise near the end of the meeting and say something very *in*, like "I think I hear you saying . . ." or "Could I ask a simple question—what are we trying to achieve?" Invariably nobody can answer the latter question and it will resonate like an echo chamber, despite the fact that, instead of listening for two hours, you've been fantasizing a febrile dalliance with the nubile corresponding secretary, Yetta Ferbrants. It is vital to hold your comment to the *closing* minutes of the meeting. Too early and you'll be named chairman of a committee on scope to find the answer to your own cockamamey question. Too late and you'll be pre-empted by the minister's closing benediction, in which he gives God a pear-shaped seven-point rebuttal of the meeting.

Another trick of surviving meetings is to develop a cer-

tain cranky shtik which gives you a special distinction. For
example, a woman from Scottsdale, Arizona—who was
definitely overworkshopped—gave up smoking after going
on a "stop smoking" cruise to the Bermuda Triangle. Thereafter, at the opening of every meeting of every organization
to which she belonged, she raised her hand and, smiling
sweetly, said: "Chairperson, I wonder if we could have a
ban on smoking at this meeting or, at least, establish a non-
smoking section like the airlines do?" At this, the whole
room goes up in smoke, what with angry speeches about
civil liberties, freedom, Castro Cuba and Havana cigars and
the right of free choice, laced with personal testimony by
newly converted nonsmokers (no one is as passionate as a
new convert) and medical testimony by cigar-smoking doctors, divisions of the house, challenging the chairperson's
ruling, calling the roll and tabling the motion. Amid the absolute futility of dealing with this simple question (the
nearer to home, the more impossible the solution), the
Committee to Feed the World's Hungry or the Committee
Against Selling Out Taiwan breaks up in a minor pogrom,
during which the lady who started it all slips out the side
door to meet her husband who wouldn't be caught dead at
any meeting not redeemed by dirty movies but fully respects
his wife's weakness.

### Negative Snobbery (NS)

One of the chic games we play is NS—Negative Snobbery.
Instead of keeping up with the Joneses in the accumulation
of possessions, practitioners of NS get brownie points for
things we wouldn't *deign* to own. The woman gets three

brownie points for *not* having a fur coat . . . four if she can afford one. The couple gets seven points for having *no* automobile . . . three for one *little* car, six if it's more than five years old, foreign, and has at least 100,000 miles on it. You get ten points for living without a telephone and thirteen for no television. And it rises to fifteen if, at a party, you show you are so rarefied you don't know Johnny Carson from Raquel Welch. The ultimate jackpot for NS is ZPG—Zero Population Growth—meaning zip children, proving we are true sophisticates who refuse to contribute to overpopulation in an ecologically rotten world. In short, NS is marvy and gives us a chance to be truly superior, especially if we can make three cups of tea (glasses even better) with one teabag.

### Choo Choo

Drs. Robert Ravich and Peter H. Wyden have come up with a gas of a game in the form of a test called "The Train Game." Two people, usually husband and wife, are given some toy electric trains to play with. Their sets are hidden from each other, but they can discuss moves and observe each other's facial expressions. Their comments are taped. Their true relationship is revealed in the game. Ravich insists he can tell when partners will or should split, which couples will hack it or which will be derailed, where there are conflicts, too much togetherness, jealousy, one-track minds, the works.

Two young scientists at Carleton College did a variation on the Choo Choo. Instead of going to all that trouble with the toy trains, they merely installed an invisible camera and a tape in the autos of fifty couples and monitored the interaction of these couples while driving in the car. In thirty-nine cases, the husband automatically got behind the wheel. Why not the wife? In interviewing the couples, it turned out not to be male chauvinism at all. The women preferred to ride their husbands than to drive the vehicles. Most of them ground their high heels into the floorboard, covered their eyes in horror every five minutes, directed the robot behind the wheel, ventilated the emotions of the day, and brought the dangerous machine, as well as the car, to a safe landing.

### Chutzpah

Another game is Chutzpah, which is a combination of cockiness and audacity. For example, your chutzpadik cousin from Chelm calls you up and asks for $300 to bury his father. Of course, you comply. But every week, thereafter, you get a bill for $19.75 for "additional funeral expenses." After a few weeks of this, you blow your stack and demand an explanation for the added money. "Oh," he replies, "you remember that Papa always wanted to be buried in a tuxedo? Well, of course, he didn't own a tux . . . so we rented one." That's chutzpah!

### Multiple Juggling

Another game is Multiple Juggling. The important thing is to do as many things at one time as humanly possible. One of the keenest practitioners of MJ was able, simultaneously, to watch TV, listen to music on the stereo, read a book, eat peanuts, drink a martini, iron clothes, telephone Mama, and shave her legs, without missing a stroke . . . which came later, felling her one hot afternoon, but from which she recovered in two weeks. Multiple Juggling is very helpful because life is too short to go forward taking one short step at a time. One must leap on all fours. And trying to do five or six things at one time guarantees that one will succeed in *nothing*, but it also provides an acceptable and ready-made excuse for *failure*. Shoot high, else what's a heaven for? My favorite MJ freak—myself—has been known to drive a car, listen to the radio, smoke a cigar, dictate a book into a tape, and compose shady limericks at one foul swoop.

### WOSD

*Waiting for the Other Shoe to Drop (WOSD)*. This game is played by masochists who get their kicks out of self-flagellation. You write a letter to the IRS, returning your form blank, saying "not one penny for tribute until the government stops pouring its money into the Pentagon rathole." Then you wait, in delicious and dreadful expectation, for the other shoe to drop—a visit from the local gendarme, a letter from Washington, a bug on your phone, a fiery cross on your lawn, or an award from the kooky Maoist Club in the posh suburb.

WOSD is a titillating game. It gives spice to life and vitality to ulcers. Henry Kissinger made himself a staple on the cover of *Time* by playing WOSD. So why can't *you*?

### BS Factor

In all games we play, it is vital to discount the all-important BS Factor. This factor plays a dominant role in international diplomacy, domestic politics (it eclipsed all else in both the Vietnam war and the Watergate debacle), but it also functions very strongly in our interpersonal relations, coloring the games we play.

You will recall that during US involvement in the Vietnam war, the BS Factor resulted in an entirely new American language, which had to be translated into common English. Some examples:

"There's light at the end of the tunnel." (We don't know where we're going, so any course will get us there, and the light in the tunnel is an express train coming *at* us!)

"We have definitely turned a corner." (Will the last guy out of Vietnam turn off the lights?)

"We must not turn our backs on the valiant free government of South Vietnam." (Don't turn your back; they'll steal us blind.)

"Our bombing of North Vietnam is a neat surgical operation." (Thank God they can't hit us with a malpractice suit.)

"We had to destroy the village in order to save it." (Sheet, we wiped out the wrong village, nobody's perfect.)

### BS Factor in Watergate

Also, the ordeal of Watergate gave us an entire new vocabulary which, coming on the heels of Vietnam, debased the language for at least a generation. Some luminous examples:

"We have been completely forthcoming." (Wild horses couldn't drag the truth out of us.)

"Stonewall it." (Lie!)

"These White House associates were the most dedicated public servants I have ever known." (These shmucks know where the bodies are buried.)

"I hear the voice of the people." (We've bugged 'em.)

"Persuade him." (Make him an offer he can't refuse.)

"Sell him on our program." (Buy him off.)

"Explain the delicacy of the situation." (Sic the IRS on him.)

"Encourage him to cooperate." (I have him on tape.)

"I am not a crook." (I *am* a crook.)

"Of course we made some mistakes of judgment." (Ask not what I can do for my country; ask what can my country do for *me!*)

"We are the first to admit that we made some mistakes." (Getting caught.)

"As the President, I and I alone must take full responsibility." (Let Mitchell take the rap.)

"Let's try that scenario again." (Play it again, John.)

"We must protect the confidentiality and privacy of White House conversations." (What *you* don't know won't hurt *us*.)

"The President has complete confidence in the judicial system." (How do I fire the Supreme Court?)

"The public is behind me." (Ten telegrams from Rabbi Baruch Korff.)

"We welcome a full investigation." (You really know how to hurt a guy.)

"The President is not allowing Watergate to distract him from urgent matters of State." (Who's playing on TV?)

"That statement is now inoperative." (That lie has been replaced by a new lie.)

"Watergate is only one page in an otherwise constructive chapter of this Administration." (They're gonna throw the book at us.)

"I have decided that political conditions . . ." (I quit, they got me!)

In our personal relations, most of us are not capable of reaching the depths of distortion of our recent leaders, but our BS Factor is working too, as, for example:

### At the Office

The telephone in your office rings. Your secretary picks it up, rolls her eyes toward you, says: "Just a moment and I'll see if he's in," muffles the mouthpiece and whispers: "It's your friend Morris Monivil. He's called ten times. Want to talk to him?"

"No," you snap. "Tell him I'm on sabbatical, tell him I'm dead, tell him I've been traded to BBD&O for a bosomy copy-writer and an old Xerox machine, tell him I've been indicted as a secret fruitarian, tell him anything, but get rid of that nudnik."

She picks up the phone, chats briefly, cups the phone again and says: "He heard you on the Long John show and just wants to tell you you were terrific."

"Hello there, Morris," you shout into the phone. "Long time no see. How nice to hear your voice again, you old sonofabitch."

The BS Factor. You can't live without it.

Or:

### At Home

You come home from the office hot and tired and ready for a shower, a Bloody Mary, and the Cronkite news. But your wife meets you at the door, reminding you that you promised to have dinner with the Palavers.

"Oh, geez, I forgot. Sure it's tonight?"

"Yes, I'm sure."

"Do we have to go to that dingaling?"

"Yes, we promised," she replies.

"Look, honey, I forgot to tell you—I have a nasty headache, bad day at the office. Be a dear and get us off the hook, while I start the race between aspirin and Bufferin."

"You know, darling, what you're full of? The BS Factor."

*Chapter XII*   **LIVING WITH A NEUROTIC (if you call that living)**

Our culture produces a bumper crop of neurotics. A neurotic is someone who isn't daffy enough to be institutionalized, but is disturbed enough to drive you right up the wall if you happen to be joined at the hip to one of them. Our culture presses us to be successes, rich, champions, young and good-looking, and while Americans have no monopoly on warped psyches, we have more than our fair share of people with flipped wigs.

Your problem may well be that you live with a neurotic person at home or at work. Inability to cope with such a relationship can fill you with guilt, rage, and self-pity. To understand the dynamic of this relationship, read *How to Live with a Neurotic* by Albert Ellis. This book will show you how to handle the neurotic . . . never "down" him, don't criticize him directly, make allowance for his problems . . . without destroying yourself. For example, Ellis teaches us how to recognize a neurotic (one who acts "illogically, inappropriately, and childishly"); and how to deal with the realities of the situation. Ellis spells out the "ABCs of Anti-Awfulling," which is a technique to help us realize that the world won't come to an end just because our partner can't make a decision or lives in terror of what other people think. This is known as "keeping things in perspective."

## Who Did What to Whom?

Ellis' approach is no doubt helpful, but it omits the key question. What made your mate neurotic in the first place? Maybe it wasn't Hollywood, TV, free enterprise, or the energy crisis. Maybe it was YOU. Maybe you are even more of a blooming freak than he/she is and maybe it was your hang-ups that freaked your mate out to begin with.

Firstly, why did you pick that particular mate or boss if it didn't satisfy your own warped need? Maybe you like to be a bastard and you picked a mate who likes to be bastardized. Maybe you picked a mate who stammers so you COULD be sure to dominate the conversation. The Vorspan Theory of Complementary Neuroses (VCN) explains a hell of a lot more than Doc Ellis' Semantic Therapy (it's enough to make a person antisemantic).

Also, why do you hang in there if you are so miserable? There is no law that says you have to continue working for a boss who likes to instruct his staff each morning in the men's room, barking out directions from his perch inside the stall. Where is it written that, if your mate insists on beating his drums at three o'clock every morning, you have to lie in bed and bear it? According to Ellis, the 3 A.M. drum-beating ritual is not the end of the world. He says you could get a night job or walk the dog. True, but it may be the end of your night's sleep and you don't have to become a spooky insomniac to make peace with a neurotic.

You could also hoist your mate with his own petard by totaling him with his own drumsticks and/or you could just split.

On the other hand, neurotics don't have to be a pain in the behind. Neurotics can also be *fun*. One of my neurotic friends is a hypochondriac and constantly pops aspirin. We place bets—win, place, and show—on whether the aspirin, Bufferin, or the Bayer will get to his bloodstream first. Another friend was obsessed with a foolish fear of trains and we bought him a third rail for his birthday. One of my early bosses was a zany who used to keep the agency files under the rug of his office, and we delighted in sweeping thumbtacks, white mice, Elmer's glue, and night crawlers under the rug each night to make each day an adventure. And who can forget how the officers on Mr. Roberts' U.S.S. *Reluctant* whiled away the dreary months in the wartime Pacific urinating in the neurotic captain's beloved flowerpot?

But, lest we yield to our sadistic impulses in shaming the neurotic, let us take a cool, hard look at *you*. Your gourd is not on so solidly either. The unexamined life is not worth living and your life can bear some examining. Why do you wear knickers to the PTA meeting? Why do you put a staple in your left ear? How come you blush when somebody tells a dirty joke? Why do you laugh uproariously when you don't get the point of a joke? Why do you have such an acute sense of smell that you can detect a Right Guard across a crowded room? Why do you eat corn on the cob so rapidly that you sound like an electric typewriter? How many times are you going to read *The Joy of Sex* and persuade yourself you like the Japanese art? Why do you feel guilty when the guard at the museum looks at you while you're looking at a Rembrandt?

How do you explain the fact that you are absolutely unable to return a purchase to the store? Why do you insist upon keeping a newspaper in your lap while sitting in the barber chair, particularly since you are bald as an egg and can't read a word without the glasses you have stuffed in your pocket?

You are, as a matter of fact, quite a neurotic mess yourself and it would be the beginning of wisdom to feel a bit less superior to your bewildered mate.

### Trashy Correspondence

Speaking of neurotics, I happened to come into possession of an intriguing and relevant correspondence between a young woman named Patsy and her parents. In this post-Watergate era of full disclosure, I feel constrained to reveal that I discovered these letters in the process of examining the contents of my neighbor's trash the other evening, while doing some free-lance piecework for the CIA. You might say that this is another illustration of garbage in, garbage out. To me, however, it recalls the pithy words of Saint Teresa, that fifteenth-century mystic, who said, "The mind is an unbroken horse." By horsing around with my neighbor's trash, I make sure there are no commies on the block and also get insightful intelligence on the state of my neighbor's mind, as the following correspondence, slightly stained by tartar sauce, demonstrates:

Dearest Patsy:

Well, it seems like years ago, but it is only three hours, that Dad and I dropped you at the airport and watched you take off, with tears in our eyes, just like when you went off to college in Michigan . . . only this time it's for keeps!!!

By now you are already in New York City, checked into the Barbizon Hotel for Women (Dad says there are *two* Barbizons; be sure you're at the one for *women*) and preparing for your first day at the job tomorrow morning. Dad and I are so proud that you have been hired as a librarian at the New York Public Library. Is that where the lions are or Teddy Roosevelt, speaking softly and carrying a big stick? Dad says it's Teddy, but he hasn't been right in twenty-seven years—since he married me. By the way, how do you know that the New York bankers won't close down the library or sell it to Rockefeller? Be sure to write every day and call on Sunday after 11 P.M.—it's only twelve cents a minute.

We want to give you some advice, please don't get angry. In looking for an apartment, find a safe street. I heard Seventy-fourth Street, on the east side, is safe but that was a month ago. And get a mature, reliable roommate. You are no longer a foot-loose coed; you are now a full-fledged college graduate, a mature young woman, beginning a career. I remember my first day in my career (I was what you call a late bloomer), which was wiped out by meeting your Dad before the career ever got flying. I'm not the bra-burner type, but I always do wonder what heights I could have scaled if I had progressed as a teller at Chase Manhattan instead of meeting that "kiss and teller" and eloping to Atlantic City. It was the dumbest thing I ever did.

                                                                    Mom


Dear Mommy:

Well, I took a cab from Kennedy, as you told me to, so please rush me more money. I checked into the Barbizon Hotel for Women and right away saw a notice on the bulletin board that someone was looking for a roommate on 103rd and Broadway. I went up there and met the someone, who turns out to be a cute guy named Aldo Vincenzi. He is very nice and says it is very unliberated of me to call you Mommy and we should call you Midge. Aldo says he likes slow horses and fast women. He sends regards.


Dearest Patsy:

We are very upset by your letter and we plan to rush to New York tomorrow, barring we reach you by phone first. What do you mean you are living with a strange man . . . and I do mean strange? I presume you are still a virgin, at least we did not hear to the contrary, and we do not care what Mrs. Ford says. Move out before it is too late. As your father is walking proof, a man is a man and they are all the same, as they are out for what they can get (which is you in trouble) and, meanwhile, put a double lock on your bedroom door and wear your Michigan sweater at night. I'm not wild about your calling me Midge, but this is the twentieth century and what's in a name? Milton is not so liberated, he choked on his veal chop when reading your letter and I had to burp him. He wants to know Aldo's religion, is it Mafia, and what do his father and godfather do.

Mom

Dear Midge:

Aldo is very nice, but he is somewhat unusual. He talks to himself and, when I ask him why, he says he is a native New Yorker. He is also a movie freak and has seen *Jaws* five times and, as a result, he will not go into any body of water whatsoever, including the bathtub.

He also likes to imitate the great stars like Jimmy Cagney and Humphrey Bogart and once, before going to bed, he got a little carried away with his Chester Morris and shot out all the lights. He and his friends eat nothing but linguine and clam sauce and salad made from zucchini he grows on the fire escape. Also, he is an interior decorator and is decorating our pad as a scene in the movie *Gaslight*. What was that about? He's a barrel of laughs and it is all platonic. Do you think Aldo is *neurotic?* How can I *tell?*

Patsy dear:

If he is a neurotic, I am reading fast as possible a book (thank the Lord I took speed-reading), *How to Live with a Neurotic.* You should definitely *not* confront him or criticize him. Let sleeping dogs lie, no matter how dirty. Whatever his mishegas, Dr. Ellis stresses that it is NOT THE END OF THE WORLD. I don't agree with Ellis, but HE is the expert. I hope Aldo at least sponge-bathes.

Here is how you will know if he is neurotic. Ask him.
Ask him especially if he says "yes" when he means "no."
Ask him if he has the inability to say "yes." Ask him does
he make eye contact. Ask him does he assert himself. Ask if
he is intimidated by waiters, conductors, and cops. For example, who picks his clothes? Ask him also if he feels *he* is
OK and *other* people are not OK or whether, like your
weird father, he thinks the whole world is out to screw him.
You could ask him how many cylinders he is truly operating on.

All OK here, but our Mazda stopped humming. I'm
worried sick about you; you are killing me. What did I do
to deserve this anguish? What did I not do for you? What
did I spare you excepting only the rod?

Midge

Dear Midge:

Aldo says you're laying a guilt trip on me and you should
cool it. I gave him your neurotic test. "Aldo, do you say
YES when you mean NO?" "Yes," he said, and I didn't
know what he meant. "Do you also say NO when you mean
YES?" "No," he replied, meaning YES.

"Do you avoid eye contact?" I asked. "No," he replied,
meaning YES, as he suddenly went into his Chester Morris
routine and shot out the lights again. "Do you assert yourself, Aldo?" I persisted. "Yes," he said, meaning NO.
"Aldo, you need assertiveness training," I suggested. "Up
yours," he replied.

Aldo and I are beginning to communicate better, even

though he is probably mildly neurotic, especially when he becomes Marie Dressler and gets into my dresses while watching the Late, Late Show.

Dear Patsy:

We can't sleep. Aldo is definitely a neurotic and you may be in danger at this very hour. Couldn't you move to East Seventy-fourth Street? It would be closer to the library lions and you wouldn't have to be kept up all night by the Late Show. Meanwhile, definitely keep your dresses under lock and key! Aldo sounds violent. I don't like guns, even for putting out the lights. Dad once went hunting and he shot off his big toe, that's why he sleeps in those dumb thongs. If that dirty Mafia Aldo so much as lays a finger on you, Milton will break his leg . . . Aldo's, I mean. Milton is a coward, but a bathless godfather in drag who is trying to decorate his daughter's interior is a horse of a different color.

You have twelve hours to move before we do!

Mom

Dear Midge and Milt:

You don't know me, but I am the person who has been living with your daughter for the past three months. I don't know how to tell you this, but your daughter is a psychological basket case and I can no longer live with a neurotic, never mind your Dr. Ellis. She loses everything that is not nailed down. She has a memory like a sieve. She actually keeps her dresses under lock and key and sleeps in a dirty

Michigan sweater. She can't speak in the morning until she has three cups of coffee inside her, and she reminds me of Ingrid Bergman in *Gaslight,* if not Olivia de Havilland in *Snakepit.* She should be in the hands of a shrink with strong nerves.

I am sure that the apple does not fall far from the tree and that you and your Milton are both nutty as fruitcakes. So *YOU* tell her—I don't have the guts—that I am splitting because you got to be crazy to live with a neurotic, if you are not married to it, especially one who is so dumb she doesn't even know that Don Ameche invented the telephone.

P.S. Me, I have found a pad on East Seventy-fourth Street in a safe neighborhood and I hope to exorcise the dybbuk of your cockamamey daughter and find peace of mind here until the very last moment when New York City is sold at auction.


Dear Aldo:

Good riddance! So you are moving to Seventy-fourth Street? There goes the neighborhood!

Do you know what Patsy said when we told her on the phone why you had split? We quote: "Good, nobody can learn to live with a neurotic."

Relieved Parents


Dearest Midge:

I have the greatest news to share with you! I know that you and Aldo have been in touch, and I'm glad you are getting to know each other. It is true that he is neurotic, but let's face it, it takes one to *know* one.

When Aldo split, I found that I missed him desperately. I couldn't sleep without the Late, Late Show and the naked bulbs filled me with nostalgia. Maybe I'm neurotic too, but the world is crazy and Aldo and I seem to complement each other's craziness. So we're eloping to Atlantic City and will spend our honeymoon at the Old Movie series at the Traymore, after which we will move into Aldo's new pad on Seventy-fourth Street which is being decorated as Stillman's Gym from *The Harder They Fall*. I've never been so happy and I know in my bare bones that Aldo will be just as good a husband as Milton has been to you all these years.

P.S. Guess how I found Aldo? I found zucchini growing on a fire escape on Seventy-fourth Street and, peeking inside, my heart pounded as I saw Marie Dressler shooting out the light bulbs. Our reunion was *not* platonic and, we are definitely compatible, what can I tell you? Aldo says he only wishes he could watch our big scene in instant replay.

P.P.S. Isn't real life crazy?

Love and kisses,
Patsy

Patsy and Aldo learned to hack it together, despite their neuroses. It should give us pause. Dr. Ellis tries to tell us how to live with a neurotic in the house and/or the office. Nervously, is the answer. But how do we know if the person is really *neurotic?* How do we know it isn't *you* that's flaking off the wall? And could it not be that we are *all* a little touched and the difference among us is just a matter of the degree to which we list to leeward?

### VNI

Following is the definitive Vorspan Neurotic Inventory (VNI) which will tell you where *YOU* stand (the time is *now* to sit down and see where you stand):

A. When people near you at the movie disturb you, you
    1. change your seat.
    2. gag them.
    3. suffer the fools gladly.
    4. demand your money back.
    5. drop a smokebomb under them.

B. The New York *Times* on Sunday represents to you
    1. an all-day project, who can finish it?
    2. a possible hernia, who can lift it?
    3. a disaster if you can't get one, even for three dollars, in Salt Lake City.
    4. the crossword puzzle.

C. When you have to stand in line, you
    1. growl a lot.
    2. whistle a merry tune.
    3. talk to your neighbor.
    4. feel sorry for yourself.
    5. always forget to take a number.

D. When people drop in unannounced, you
    1. are delighted to see them.
    2. hide under the bed.
    3. slip out the back door and go to a neighborhood saloon.

E. A telephone ring signifies to you
    1. a new adventure.

    2. a damned intrusion.

    3. a bill collector.

F. You like people who

    1. like you.

    2. are cheerful.

    3. agree with your politics.

    4. stay in books where they belong.

G. You gave up smoking

    1. fifty times.

    2. to safeguard your health.

    3. because you burned up most of your clothes.

H. To you, dining alone in a restaurant is

    1. an impossible bore.

    2. bearable only if you have a newspaper or a book.

    3. a grand opportunity to stare at strangers and eavesdrop on their conversations.

    4. not deductible as entertainment.

    5. so nerve-racking you choke on your kasha.

I. What you think about most of the time is

    1. food.

    2. sex.

    3. whatever the last person you spoke to said.

    4. what's on TV.

J. When you die, you would like to be

    1. buried.

    2. remembered.

    3. cremated.

    4. surprised.

K. When someone criticizes you, you

    1. take it in a constructive spirit.

    2. develop a tic.

    3. say: "You're another."

L. You feel depressed when

    1. the weather is bad.

    2. the weather is good.

    3. you meet somebody who is in a cheerful mood.

M. In your family, sibling rivalry is

    1. nonexistent, you're close as thieves.

    2. sublimated, you *are* thieves.

    3. keen, you need buffer zones and bataca bats.

    4. none of your business, don't make trouble.

N. When someone compliments you, you

    1. blush.

    2. quickly return the compliment.

    3. ask that it be repeated.

Here's how you score the VNI. There are no "correct" answers—each is a matter of opinion. The purpose of the test is to measure your *behavior,* not your *answers.* For example, if you quit before you started, you are uncurious, suffer from lack of discipline, and/or are afraid to compete. This is exceedingly neurotic, and is a no-no and your score is *zip*.

On the other hand, if you plowed on to the very end, despite everything and muttering angrily to yourself, you are equally neurotic, suffering from excessive intimidation by authority (me) and compulsive personality (you). You are a harmless example of the Nuremberg Syndrome—doing what you are told, no matter what. In a recent scientific test, subjects were told to apply ever stronger doses of electrical shock to another subject upon instruction of the scientist—and most of them just kept turning up the juice until the other party would have been fried sunny side up! If you answered *all* these nutty questions, you also get *zip*.

The *mature* personality, on the other hand, did about nine or ten and then asked himself: "What kind of craziness is this? I'm bailing out." If you quit in the middle, you are a middling, mediocre personality, lacking neuroses but also couth.

### Eleven* Commandments for a Neurotic Life-Style

1. Never do *today* what you can put off until *tomorrow*. Procrastination is the mother of invention.
2. If at first you don't succeed, *blame* your mother and father.
3. *Cover* your behind. This means putting a memo in the file and the blame on someone else.
4. The law of survival is an *I* for an *I,* and look out for Number One.
5. Do it to *him* before he does it unto *you*.
6. Just because you are slightly *paranoid* doesn't mean that they are *not* out to screw you.
7. *Live* every day as if it were your *last*. Return overdue library book.
8. It is true that you should not covet thy neighbor's ass, but who can ignore the tight sweater?
9. Nobody stubs his toe on a mountain. It is the *pebbles* which drive us crazy.
10. Wake up each morning with a grin and ask: "Is *this* all there is to life?"
11. *Kvetch* and the whole world will *kvetch* with you.

* Enlarged by inflation.

# EPILOGUE

We live in times of angst and ennui, which is a lot better than the times of Ehrlichman and Haldeman. To say we are uncertain about tomorrow is an understatement; we are uncertain there will even *be* a tomorrow. Change, sudden and sometimes violent, convulses our lives. Meanwhile, the time-honored foundations on which previous generations built their lives—family, faith, work, the American ideal—seem to be collapsing around our ears.

What is there to believe in? How can we cope? Must we rediscover the wheel? How can we impose some meaning on the absurdity of our lives? With whom can we interface? How can we earn our space on this planet? Who knows? So, we thrash about for an anchor to windward, a solid rock amid the quicksands, something that will explain the inexplicable. We look for instant salvation and we find "panaceas" everywhere . . . in astrology, witchcraft, encounter groups, messianic religious groups, revolution, headshrinkers, gurus, macrobiotic foods, vegetarianism, or whatever form of psychbooby and future shlock will seem to make us feel better.

It wouldn't help.

### Snake Oil

Life is a struggle, but the only escape from its perils is the
cemetery. Life may well be absurd, but absurd over-
simplifications only make US absurd. Psychic acupuncture
may perforate us; it doesn't heal us. There is no easy, simple
answer to the enigmas and mystery of human life. Having
our credulity raped and our anxieties stroked brings us no
closer to maturity. The enigmas and mysteries, transcending
our limited powers, are part of our very humanity. If we
trade in the struggle in exchange for some cheap and facile
certitude, we trivialize the struggles that give character to
our lives. The self-help formula, at bottom, is usually a recipe for cop-out. It is a mod version of snake oil and leeches.
Better the long, hard road than the quick shortcut leading
only to garbage in and garbage out.

Besides, why do you want to be your own best friend?
Who said you have to be "OK"? Why learn to live with another person when you can't stand yourself? Why should we
be "kind" to ourselves? Why is it better to be a "winner"
than a "loser"? Is it so important to be absolutely certain
that one possesses the whole and eternal truth? What
wrongs have been committed by those possessing absolute
certitude!

Remember the statement of Oliver Cromwell: "I beseech
ye, in the bowels of Christ . . . consider that ye may be
mistaken." Where is it written you have to be a happy yo-
yo all your life?

Personally, I prefer the company of an unsure, mixed-up,
funky, ambivalent, cantankerous, and mildly neurotic friend

to one for whom all life is a proof text for a preconceived notion. Spare me the company of those who have already figured it all out. Better one day in hell with someone for whom life is a daily challenge, conundrum, wonder, and sometimes a pain in the tush—but who maintains a capacity to laugh at it and himself—than a thousand days in the courts of the smug know-it-alls.

Well, now you have it. We've tried to extract whatever sap there is in these here trees, but—still—we can't see the forest for the trees. Some of these books were more gainful for the publishers than helpful to us readers. Some are heady rip-offs. A few have some good common sense in them, padded and inflated into great truths.

But no one of them—nor all of them gulped down together with A.1. Sauce—will provide the quick fix we seem to be seeking. So what's the answer? When Gertrude Stein lay dying, she is alleged to have been asked that question by her devoted buddy, Alice Toklas. Stein replied: "What is the question?" and expired. Think about that.

### A Biblical Time

We are living at a time akin to the Biblical moment in Deuteronomy when God said: "I have placed before you life and death, the blessing and the curse, so why shall ye die? Choose life and live."

We need to choose life—as individuals, determined to grow in love and in self-understanding! But also as human beings, responsible to and for the shape of the larger society. We need to take the world and put it on the anvil of life —and beat it into a more humane shape. In the process we may also safeguard our own humanity. Despair about America and the world is a cop-out. Each day is a new page for each of us to devour. If we are too jaded or too frantic to read the page, we are really illiterate, even if we have a Ph.D. in English Literature.

Since much that happens in the world is insane and absurd, we need to maintain our sense of humor if we are to retain our sanity. We laugh in order not to cry. We enjoy the absurdities of life in order to stay human in an inhuman time. Humor is a saving grace. In our time, it is an essential ingredient of our personal survival kit. A Charlie Chaplin, W. C. Fields, or Woody Allen is a greater tonic for our souls than a hundred pompous politicians spraying us with bombast. Life is real and life is serious, yes, and we do not laugh in order to devalue its significance.

Another essential for survival is to persist, despite everything, in improving the world. One of the sins of the self-help mystique is that it often turns off the outside world and ignores our social and moral responsibility to society at large. Working on one's own head is OK, but how can a person find *peace* if the house is falling down around him? How can one contemplate his own navel while half a billion people face sheer famine on the same planet—and still be *human?* How can one recite his mantras or play with his tarot cards while society makes the elderly, the poor, and the minorities the helpless victims of economic suffering? What good is finding one's "identity" if the culture is infected with a gun-craziness and you can be mugged or savaged for the crime of walking to the nearest deli? Self-help, without social concern, is pure narcissism. A Ralph Nader, giving himself to advancing social justice and saving the environment, is more alive than ten thousand dingalings exploring their astrology charts while neglecting the pain of their neighbors. And Nader probably has fewer identity problems than any of us who have spent our lives as wistful ciphers seeking the Holy Grail and the one true nostrum to life!

The current passion for self-help is, to some extent, a measure of political exhaustion and despair. But we cannot afford despair. America and the world have never been in more desperate need of persons who *care,* who are capable of compassion and empathy, and who have the *courage* to act for decency, equality, justice, and peace. Such persons may save the world—and, in the process, discover their inner selves.

An ancient rabbi once said, "It is not incumbent upon us to complete the task; but neither are we free to desist from it."

That ancient rabbi was a mensch who had his head on straight and he didn't need a bataca bat, an orgone box, or tarot cards to do it!

*Please return to*
*Nancy Taylor*